"For The Love of Old Glory"

An Autobiography by
John Ben Worley

Library of Congress Cataloging in Publication Data Worley, John B.
For The Love of Old Glory
Library of Congress Catalog Number: Pending
Cover Layout, Typography and Editing: Jon Sharp
Vertigo Creative Concepts
McCamey, Texas
www.vertigocreative.com

PHOTO CREDITS:
"Hitler and Mussolini in Munich, Germany, ca. June 1940." is a public domain photo from the Eva Braun Collection at the National Archives and Records Administration
Bob Hope & Frances Langford photo courtesy of Rob at www.thewarpage.com
Miscellaneous public domain World War II photos courtesy of the United States Army Center of Military History - http://www.army.mil/cmh-pg/
ISBN 0-7414-1337-X

Published by:

519 West Lancaster Avenue
Haverford, PA 19041-1413
Info@buybooksontheweb.com
www.buybooksontheweb.com
Toll-free (877) BUY BOOK
Local Phone (610) 520-2500
Fax (610) 519-0261

Printed in the United States of America
Printed on Recycled Paper
Published November 2002

DEDICATION

I dedicate this book to my dear wife Imogene Worley who has been a dedicated wife, mother to our children, homemaker, friend, helpmate, and now a devoted grandmother for fifty years. She has had a strong influence on our children. She loved them through their youth and their teenage years. She loves people and loves to visit with everyone. She loves Odessa and West Texas. She always supported me when I had disappointments at the work place. When I was offered a job in Odessa years ago and asked her what she thought, she said she was ready to go whereever I thought I could make her and the children a living. She always accepted the paychecks that I brought home and made do until the next payday. When all of the children were old enough to go to school she took a part-time job to help out with the growing cost of living. But she always made sure she could be home when the children came home from school. She never let them stay home alone. She was a Christian when we met and she taught our children to be truthful and to have high moral standards. She also influenced them to become Christians. When we moved to Odessa we became involved in church work. I liked to go to church when I could. When I had to work she took the rest of the family to church and Sunday school. She has helped me through many dark days in my life. When I had health problems, she was there for me. When the children were sick she knew what to do. She is a good cook, a good shopper, and a good housekeeper. She likes to keep everything in its place, neat and clean.

I also dedicate this book to our four children who brought us much happiness, who were good children and still are. They have never been in trouble and we are so proud of all of their accomplishments. We encouraged them to get a college education and they took our advice and did it. They followed our guidelines on being honest, friendly and having high moral standards and loving one another.

To my grandchildren, I wish to let them know about the war and the Great Depression. I hope that they will heed their parents' training and their advice and never get involved in any illegal activities or drugs, alcohol, or tobacco. I hope they will become Christians and lead an honest and happy life.

Finally, this book is dedicated to the memory of all of my dear friends and fellow soldiers who were killed in battle and those who were buried in cemeteries in Italy. They did not get to come home to their loved ones or live a long and happy life as I did. They gave their lives for our country so that we could be with our sweethearts, raise our families, go to church, and give thanks to God for a good life. I think of them often. They are my heroes.

John B. Worley

Preface

John Ben Worley doesn't like to hear me call him a hero. But after hearing this story of his life I can't help myself. He has become one of my heros. John was born on a farm near Lindsay, Oklahoma, on November 28th, 1921 to honest, hard working, sharecroppers Jack & Blanche Worley. His was a classic southern childhood during the hard times of the Great Depression and the Dust Bowl. John was the fourth child of six and recalls fondly that his parents taught all of their children to work hard and, above all else, to be honest.

His early life shaped him into the patriotic man he is today. Some of those experiences included helping his mother with her chores at the age of five, working in the fields and keeping up with grown men when he was ten, and joining the National Guard simply to earn some spending money when he was seventeen. But John soon found that he would get more out of the Guard than spending money. Before he knew it, the National Guard was mobilized into the regular army and was moved to Fort Sill, Oklahoma, where John began full-time regular army training.

In this compelling memoir, John Worley recalls his amphibious ship-to-shore landing training with the 45th Infantry Division. It was this training which equipped John to participate in three landings on Nazi-occupied beaches: on the Island of Sicily on July 10th, 1943; at Salerno, Italy, on September 10th, 1943; and at Anzio, Italy, on February 3, 1944.

It was at Anzio, during a night counterattack, that a shell from a German Tiger tank struck John in the chest. In the darkness, the critically injured John Worley was pronounced dead. One brave soldier insisted, however, that John's body be carried off the battle field to the first aid station a couple of miles away so he could receive a proper burial. Upon arrival the medics found that the "body" was miraculously clinging to life so John was immediately rushed to the mobile hospital on the beach. After three surgeries and two months in intensive care, he was shipped to the army hospital in Fort Sam Houston at San Antonio, Texas. Finally, after five months in the Army Hospital, John was discharged from the U.S. Army he loved without being asked or given any choice in the matter.

Unwillingly leaving all of his friends in the army, John went home to his parents. He quickly became depressed due, in part, to his continuing pain and his inability to work or help his parents around their farm. The depression was worsened by his neighbors' lack of respect for the war and for those who fought and gave their lives for our nation's freedom. His parents and family were the only ones who really cared when he told of his experiences, listening in awe to the shocking stories of the fighting and the deaths of John's buddies. Soon after his discharge from the army, John met Imogene, the prettiest girl he had ever seen. They were married the following year and she has remained his life-long sweetheart, helpmate, and companion.

Imogene helped bring John out of his depressed state of mind with her patience and happy disposition and helped him to focus on the future. Together, they raised a wonderful, loving family of one boy and three

4

girls.

After a period of telling and retelling the same stories over and over, and worrying that he was boring his listeners, he came to believe that if he did not speak about it, those painful memories might go away. Fifty years later, after waking up in a cold sweat after a nightmare, he realized that the memories of the War and his good friends who died overseas were still vivid in his mind.

John continued to keep his stories, his memories, his pain, to himself until very recently when Curtis Brewer, the Music Minister of their church, asked John to give his testimony at a Fourth of July Patriotic Celebration program. Though painful and difficult, John Worley shared some of the long silent memories and afterwards, felt the relief that comes from sharing with people who, especially in these times of increased Patriotism, wanted to hear his story. That experience helped him decide to write about his childhood during the Great Depression, his World War II experiences, and his fascinating life after the war, which John has lived faithfully for God and Country. Anyone who has the opportunity to read this account of Mr. Worley's life should feel grateful. It is not often that we get to hear these stories anymore. The great men and women who experienced the turbulent World War II era are quickly disappearing, but John Worley has graciously shared his joy and his pain in this faithful recount of his amazing life. Through telling his story, John quietly yearns to remind every American that our freedom was bought with the blood of his friends, the real American heros who died defending our country. And I would like to remind Mr. Worley that shedding his own blood for our freedom and living to tell us about it made him a real American hero, too.

Jon Sharp
Editor, Admirer

CONTENTS

Chapter 1
The Great Depression

I was born in 1921 while we were living on the Mex Bullock farm, three miles east and one and a half miles south of Lindsay, Oklahoma. I do not remember anything that happened while we lived there, because we moved the next year to the farm just south across the road which was owned by Mex's mother, Granny Bullock. My parents had three children before I was born. My oldest brother Scott, then Seburn and my sister Emogene. We lived on Mrs. Bullock's farm until I was ten years old, and then we moved to the Scott Moore farm just half a mile east. Dad was able to rent that farm because he had three big strong boys to help him with the farm work. The Moore place was 200 acres with forty acres in timber and 160 acres of good bottomland. The other two farms were up-land. We lived there until I graduated from high school at the age of seventeen.

My dad and mom, Jack and Blanche Worley, were sharecroppers. They were strict, honest, hardworking, conservative Christian parents and they were good managers. During the Great Depression from about 1927 to 1940, it was a very good idea to be good managers. There was very little money in the entire region. There were no food stamps, no savings, no social security, no retirement funds, and very few jobs, except at harvest time. Wages for harvest hands were fifteen cents an hour. In the middle 1930's, the pay was raised to twenty cents an hour.

Mom was a good cook. We always had plenty to eat, mostly because we raised all kinds of vegetables and fruit that would grow in the Oklahoma climate. My family had a garden every year and we raised all of our food, except for spices, salt and pepper, sugar, and other things we could not plant. Dad even raised wheat and had it ground into whole-wheat flour at the mill, and he gave a portion to the miller for the grinding. He also raised corn and had it ground into cornmeal. We raised every kind of vegetable that would grow in that climate, so we had fresh vegetables all spring and summer, and my mom canned the surplus in pint, quart, and half-gallon fruit jars, which we stored in the storm cellar. Every farm in the Lindsay, Oklahoma area had a storm cellar. Our cellar was always cool in the summer and never got cold enough to freeze the canned vegetables in the winter.

We raised and butchered all of our meat including beef, pork, chicken, turkey, goose, goat, rabbit, and one time we had opossum. Dad always insisted that we have meat on the table for every meal. We always milked five or six cows and had plenty of good, sweet milk to drink. Seburn and I separated the cream from the rest of the milk and churned some for butter. Whatever cream we did not churn and whatever eggs were left over, Mom would sell to the produce store in town. We also butchered four or five fat hogs and a fat yearling calf in the winter after the weather got cold.

Dad would pick a cold day to kill hogs. We would usually have five or six fat hogs ready to butcher. I kept the fire going under the big black wash-pot. We poured the boiling water in a barrel and scalded each hog until the hair would slip, and then I helped scrape the hair off. We always had some of the neighbor men over to help and we went to help them when they butchered their hogs. Dad quartered each animal and we carried the meat into the house. Dad trimmed the hams and shoulders and sugar-cured them, and finally hung them in the smokehouse for curing and safekeeping until we ate the ribs, loins, and backbone. The fat we would trim, cut into little pieces, and put in a tub until the next day. We trimmed all the other lean meat, ground it, and made it into sausage. Sometimes it would be after midnight before we finished, but it had to be done before we quit. This was before iceboxes, deep-freezes, or air conditioners were invented.

The next morning I would start a fire under the old black washpot, and dump all the hog's fat, which had been cut into little pieces the night before, into the pot and stand by to stir it. It took about four hours to render all the grease from the cracklins. Then I dipped out the cracklins and poured the grease into five-gallon lard cans. Soon it hardened somewhat into white lard. Then I put the cracklins back in the pot, added a small amount of water and four cans of Eagle Brand lye, and continued to boil and stir until all the cracklins were dissolved by the lye. The result was a year's supply of golden yellow lye soap for laundering clothes or washing dishes.

Mom raised three or four hundred chickens every year. Some of the hens would lay their quota, then sit on the nest and hatch fifteen or twenty little chicks. She also bought 100 baby chicks from the hatchery three times per year and raised them in a brooder house, warmed by a small kerosene stove. Dad bought Mom an incubator, also fueled by kerosene. We had to keep the eggs warm and turn them over every day. Baby chicks would hatch in twenty-one days. She also hatched baby turkeys and geese, and raised them to sell in the fall and for our own food. She also raised some guineas. They were pretty wild, but they were good security. They would honk and cackle real loudly if a person or anything strange came on the place. We ate the guinea eggs and some of the fowl and sold the rest.

We had plenty of eggs to eat and out of the guineas, turkeys, geese, and chickens we raised, we would save a turkey or a goose for our Thanksgiving dinner and one for our Christmas dinner. Mom would sell the rest at the produce store in Lindsay. She would use the money she got from cream, eggs, and poultry to buy groceries and things we could not grow on the farm such as sugar, pepper, salt, and medicine. Our basic medicine was black draught, Epsom salts, Vick's salve, castor oil, and iodine and Mecurochrome and methiolate for cuts and skins. The closest hospital to us was at El Reno, Oklahoma. Seburn had appendicitis when he was twelve years old. Mom and Dad had to take him to El Reno for surgery one stormy, rainy night in the Model T. It was seventy-five miles. We had Dr. Gross in Lindsay who would make house calls if someone were really bad, but otherwise Mom and Dad used home remedies. For chest colds and deep coughs Mom put a mustard plaster on our chests and covered it with flannel cloth. Medical and surgical knowledge is fantastic today.

She also used the money to buy some clothing and the necessary things that she needed for sewing. Mom bought thread and cloth and made a lot of our clothes. She made shirts for Dad and us boys, and she made dresses for the girls. She had a foot-pedaled Singer sewing machine, and she made a lot of other things, like pillowcases, sheets, tablecloths, and much more. She also made quilts, blankets, pillows, and feather beds, which she stuffed with the down from the geese. We did not buy anything that we could raise or make at home. She also darned our socks and patched our overalls. Us boys only had 3 pairs of overalls — one pair to wear while the second pair was in the dirty clothes pile, and the third pair was blue-and-white striped, for Sunday only.

When we ran low on money for supplies, Dad would establish a credit account at the grocery store in town. In the wintertime, he made a loan at the bank for enough money to buy seed, tools, machinery, and equipment for the spring planting. Dad made an agreement to pay the grocery bill and the bank loan when the crop was harvested the next year. It was a sad day back then when someone made a promise and did not keep it. It was very seldom that anyone did that. In those days a handshake was as good as a contract on any or all deals. Dad mortgaged all of his livestock and machinery for the loan to tide us over until the first crop was harvested the following year. A crop failure would have been a disaster for us. I never knew what a strain my Dad was going through all those years until I was grown. Due to our Dad and Mother's good management and perseverance we came through those lean years in fine shape.

If Dad had not been able to pay off the debts at the grocery store and the bank each year, we might have gone to California and joined the other Okies that they wrote about in *The Grapes of Wrath*. If that had happened, then this story would have had another ending.

Life on The Farm

In the early days of my life, until about 1940, an ice cream cone, a candy bar, a package of gum, or a big bottle of Nehi soda pop cost a nickel. Baby Ruth and Butterfinger candy bars were twice as big as they are today.

In the 1920's and 1930's, the postage to send a letter to anywhere in the United States was 3 cents. A postcard only cost a penny for the one-cent stamp already on it. We mailed a lot of penny postcards. You could buy a package of cigarettes for a dime, or you could buy a can of Prince Albert tobacco for a dime and roll your own. My dad smoked Prince Albert and in the later years of his life he had respiratory problems.

Haircuts were 25 cents at the barbershop, but we did not have that much money to spare. My dad cut my hair until I started earning my own money working for the neighbor at the age of ten years.

The Saturday evening western movie at the Blue Moon Theater was ten cents, but the price of the late night "preview show" was twenty-five cents. Saturday was the only day the theater was open. All the stores closed early all other nights, because no one came to town on weekdays. They did not sell popcorn or soft drinks at the theater at all.

Our only transportation until 1927 was a wagon and team. We had three or four horses that we rode, but we mostly worked them in the field each day, pulling harvest wagons, planters, cultivators, hayracks, and other machinery. We also rode the horses to round up the cows. Dad bought his first car in 1927. It was a two-door coupe, Model-T Ford. Dad did the driving, Mom and Scott sat in the only seat with Dad, and Seburn had a little seat over the gas tank, right behind the driver's seat. Dad fixed a little seat for me and Emogene, between the back glass and the top of his seat. It was mighty cozy, but it was the best we could do. We did not go much, as I remember. (I guess because Dad did not have enough money for the gasoline.) Dad also had a one-horse buggy, the one he had when he courted Mom. Mom once took me, my Uncle Ike's first wife, and their four year-old son, Audry, for a ride in the pasture looking for turkey nests. I was four at the time.

I can remember things that happened when I was really young, and I can tell how old I was when it happened by the farm where we lived at the time. I remember a lot of things that happened while the three older children were away at school. I was five years old when I started to school.

They say you never forget your raising, and I believe that is so. I am a very conservative person and can't help it. I am very careful how I spend my money and where I can make the best buy. My dad was conservative too. He raised all the feed for our livestock. On the Bullock farm, we raised cotton, corn, sorghum, and some broomcorn besides what was in our garden. There we had a little creek bottom with a live spring. Near the spring, Dad made a trough out of bridge timber, so the livestock had good, cool water all summer and warm water in winter. At the edge of the creek bottom the soil was rich and sub-irrigated, and that was where we planted our garden. We had all kinds of fresh vegetables from early spring until frost.

I helped my mom with the garden, gathered the eggs, and built a fire under the big wash pot outside and kept the water hot for her on wash days. She put the clothes in the boiling water and she and Emogene took them out one piece at a time and scrubbed them on a washboard with our homemade lye soap.

I was assigned the job of finding the turkey and goose nests. This was before I was old enough to start school. The geese and turkey hens would try to hide their nests in the pasture or the woods, so that they could sit on the eggs and hatch little ones. The danger of wild animals eating the eggs, the little chicks, or the mother hen was too great, so my job was to stalk the hens when they left the flock without letting them see me. Mom said if they saw me or noticed anything strange, they would turn aside and go back to the flock. They would try to slip off again soon, however. When I was able to follow them without being seen, they usually led me to a clump of grass or bushes in the wooded part of the pasture.

I learned to be really sneaky at that early age, not knowing that it would be a great help to me fifteen years later in a foreign country, hiding from a crafty and deadly enemy. My mom tied a big soup spoon on the end of a long stick. After the hen laid her egg, I reached into the nest with the spoon on the stick and took out the egg. Mom said if the hen smelled any strange scent or even saw tracks or anything different when she returned, she would leave the nest and find a new place. So I was very careful to not disturb anything. Sometimes a hen would go out to her nest but turn away and go back to the farm. I would usually find animal tracks around the nest that she left.

Mom had her incubator hatching eggs year-round. One day, a white gosling was hatched. Mom gave it to me and said it was a reward for finding the nests and helping her with the eggs and the little chicks. I was really proud of that little white goose. I watched it grow until it was half-grown. It was all feathered out and really stood out in the flock of Grey geese. One morning, the geese were grazing in a field of young corn near the house. Dad saw them and began to yell at them and wave his arms. He picked up an old bone that the dogs had been gnawing on and threw it into the flock of geese. Out of the forty-some geese, the bone hit the white one and killed it. So much for that! I was no longer in the goose ownership business!

I remember, when I was five, going to Grandpa and Grandma Diggs and spending a week with them and Mom's siblings, Calvin, Finley, and June. It was really nice. Grandpa had a rural telephone installed way back, sometime soon after Dad and Mom got married. They had a party line, and I would listen to the neighbors gossiping on the phone. While staying there, at Grandpa's, Calvin got really sick in the night, and passed out. Dad saddled a horse and rode ten miles to Lindsay and brought back Dr. Gross. The doctor said Uncle Calvin had meningitis. Whatever it was, he finally recovered, but it crippled him for life. He had very little use of his leg, but he lived to the ripe old age of 92. Soon after his illness Calvin had a really bad argument with Grandpa and left for California, riding freight trains. After he left, I was helping Grandpa shuck some corn to feed the horses, and I found a quart fruit jar full of corn whiskey. I suspect that was the cause of the trouble between them.

Uncle Finley and Aunt June were teenagers then and went to school at Oak Grove, a first through eighth-grade school. Unknown to me, my future wife, Imogene, lived just a few yards from that school, and she would go to school there later. Uncle Finley did not feel well that week, but he would get to feeling better after Aunt June left for school. He and I would make kites and fly them. We also played down on the creek. He and Uncle Calvin had made a huge swing down there in a tall cottonwood tree. The Howard family lived just across the creek. Anna Howard would be my primary teacher the very next year at old Hughes high school, but I was not aware of that when we visited them that week.

One evening after supper, we were all sitting out in the yard on the shady side of the house. The horse lot was nearby, and the horses had already eaten. I asked Grandpa if I could ride one of his pretty bay mares. He must have thought that it was not likely that a five-year-old boy could bridle and mount one of the horses, so he said that I could ride one if I could catch her. I got the bridle from the barn and strolled out into the corral. The fence was made of poles and was about as tall as the horses' backs. I spied a mare that was standing close to the fence, so I walked up to her very slowly and easily, talking to her all the time. I stepped up on the bottom rail and eased the bit in her mouth and drew the bridle over her ears. Then I climbed up another rail and straddled her back. They were all very surprised, and Uncle Finley came out and opened the gate for me, so I could ride down the road and back. I had a great time at Grandma's house and will remember it for a long time.

Shortly after I came home from Grandma Diggs' house, Uncle Elbert Evans (we always called him Uncle Elb) came to our house in a wagon pulled by a team of beautiful dapple gray horses. He told us his mother was really sick and that they needed Mom to come and take care of her. He said it had become too much for them. Elb was an only child, probably 35 years old and never married, and he still lived at home with his parents, who were my Great-Grandpa and Grandma Evans, my mom's grandparents. They lived seven miles south of Lindsay, on the same crooked old highway as Grandma Diggs. Mom went with Uncle Elb and, since I had not started to school yet, she took me with her. Grandma Evans was very sick; she could not get out of bed or take care of herself. My guess is that she had cancer, but no one had heard of cancer way back then. Lots of people died at home in bed, and they would say, "Well, they had consumption," or "It was the plague," or something else.

People did not go to the hospital, because there wasn't one. If there were any doctoring, the country doctor would come in his horse and buggy and leave some medicine. Grandma was bed-fast for a month or so before she died. My mother took care of her all that time and cooked and cleaned house for Grandpa and Uncle Elb. One morning, Grandma told me and my mom that she awoke in the night, and someone dressed in a white robe with a shining face was standing at her bedside. Grandma said that she tried to reach out and touch the figure, but it disappeared. She died before noon that day. If ever there was a saint on earth, I believe my Great Grandma Evans was one. So were my Grandma Diggs and my Mom.

I never knew my Grandpa or Grandma Worley. Grandma died when my Dad was 12 years old. Grandpa Worley died when I was five. Dad only took Seburn with him to the funeral. Grandpa Worley was buried near Boonville, Texas.

There was a man named Ed Denson who lived on Rush Creek, about ten miles south of our place. Mr. Denson owned a lot of land. He had nine sons, and most of them lived at home or close by. They all worked the farmland for him because he was old and had already done his share. Now, Mr. Denson liked to drink corn whiskey and hunt wolves at night with his sons and his wolfhounds. Everyone said that the whiskey was going to kill Mr. Denson and it finally did; when he was 97 years old.

One morning just after sun up, Mr. Denson and all of his sons came riding down the road to our house. About a dozen hounds were trotting along with the horses. Dad went out to greet them. My dad got along real good with all his neighbors and knew everyone in the whole community because the county hired him to take the census of the school district each year. Mr. Denson told Dad that they had been hunting all night. They had been on a wolf's trail, and had lost his trail in the woods nearby about daylight. Mr. Denson told us that day that when the hounds were on a wolf's trail each dog had a different tone in their bawling. He could call them by name and tell his sons which hound struck the trail first, which one was in the lead, which was second, third, and so on, all this while sitting by a cozy fire a mile or so away. Dad invited them to dismount and come in the house, and my mom would fix them some breakfast. They tied their horses to the yard fence and went in the house. The hounds came in the yard to lay down, and were quickly sound asleep.

My brother Seburn and I were in the yard and Seburn said to me, "Why don't you go tickle one of them with that long stalk of broomcorn and see what they will do?" I thought that was a good idea, so I picked up the stalk and proceeded to rake it across the feet of the nearest wolfhound. That old dog woke up and thought he was on a hot trail. He bawled like a freight train engine at a road crossing, and all the hounds awoke and started bawling. They jumped up and took off chasing me while I took off running for the front door! Mr. Denson came out the door and yelled at the dogs just in time. They quit chasing me at once and returned to their prior positions as if nothing had happened. I learned a good lesson that day that I would not forget for years to come — LET SLEEPING DOGS LIE.

One night, my Uncle Calvin went along with the Densons on a wolf hunt. They were all sitting around a campfire while the hounds were searching the pastures and canyons nearby, trying to get the scent of a wolf's trail. Now and then, a hound would let out a lonesome bawl. Soon, one hound sounded off and all the others joined in. Mr. Denson said, "Old Blue has found a trail... Listen to the others as they find it... That sounds like music to my ears!" Uncle Calvin spoke up and said, "I can't hear the music for them darn hounds a-barking!"

One thing I remember really well from those days is lying in the floor by my father's chair after supper, listening to him sing "The Old Rugged Cross," "The Church in the Wildwood," and many others while he held my sister Emogene on his lap. I also remember that my mother read the Bible to me a lot when I was a very small boy. We did not have a church there in the country and it was too far to travel to town and back by wagon and team. However, I remember going to the Lindsay Baptist Church the night that Seburn was baptized. The pastor there was Brother Campbell, the son-in-law of Mrs. Bullock, the lady who owned the rented farm where we lived. Dad made me sit still and quiet during the service. Now I am so thankful that he taught me to be respectful in the Lord's house. "Be still and know that I am God." (Psalm 46:10). Dad had told me that the offering they took up was for God. I remember wondering how in the world they were going to get it up to heaven where He was.

When I was 9 years old, we went to Decatur, Texas, at Christmas and visited my Aunt Vineybell and Uncle Ben for a week. They were having a revival at their church that week. Aunt Vineybell was director for the youth choir and she asked me to sing in her choir. One night, while the preacher was giving the invitation, I felt a strong urge to go down and talk to him. I told him how I felt and that I knew what it meant to become a Christian. I accepted Jesus then and there, without talking to my parents first. I realized this while I stood there, and I got a little weak in the knees thinking about what my father might do to me for not asking first, but I knew it would be all right with Mom. When the invitation was over and I was presented to the church, I felt Dad's big hand on my shoulder. I thought to myself, "Here it comes. . ." I turned and Dad said, "I am proud of you, Son."

We had a two-week revival in the country each summer at one of the rural schoolhouses, Hughes High School or Snider Grade School. Either location was a long ride in a horse-drawn wagon for our family. We would attend every night after working in the field all day. There was preaching and singing of all the good gospel hymns that we still sing in church today. Things that you learn when you are young, like those songs, stay with you a long time. I would get really sleepy on the way home and lie down in the wagon on a quilt, and Mom would wake me when we got home. I was not a very strong Christian during my teenage years. The nearest Sunday regular service was in First Baptist Church in Lindsay, and that was five miles from our home. We also worked on Sunday a lot. In the spring, when the rainy season came and the weeds grew fast, and also during harvest time, this was a way of life. Dad would say, "The ox is in the ditch," meaning he felt that it was necessary to work on Sunday and that we would not be going to church.

When I was a little boy, my dad kept a watchful eye on clouds that came in the night, especially if there was thunder and lightning near by. It always seemed that all storms came at night, after I was sound asleep. Dad would wake up the family and direct us toward the storm cellar. Like I said before, all the farmhouses had storm cellars. It was a safe place to be during a storm as well as a good place to store our canned fruit and vegetables. He would usually wait until the wind started blowing from the cloud. I can still remember how sleepy I was every time we went to the cellar. I remember my dad carrying me and the wind blowing dust in my face. The wind sounded so mournful, blowing across the vent pipe. When the wind blew real strong and the rain started falling, Dad would pull the doors shut and tie it down with the rope. I always went back to sleep and was awakened again when the storm had passed over. Sometimes it would be four or five hours. In present times, we have radio and television that gives us daily weather reports and forecasts with satellite pictures of the movement of highs and lows, cloud locations, very accurate predictions of temperature, rain clouds, and high winds for the coming week. How things have changed over the years. We don't even have a storm cellar at our house now, and we usually sleep through a storm cloud unless the fire department blows a siren, signaling a possible tornado nearby.

My mom and dad were really strict about us doing what they told us to do. We were not allowed to talk back to them. They made it very clear that we were to tell the truth and mind them or we would wish that we had. There were no laws in those days to worry parents about child abuse charges. The parents had full responsibility and authority over their children at home. The superintendent and schoolteachers were responsible for our conduct at school. The punishment for most misdemeanors was a paddling by the teacher or the superintendent. Students were expelled for more serious conduct. At our house it was a whipping with a razor strap, a check line, or a tree limb. Dad made it very clear that if we got a whipping at school, we would get another one when we got home. As I look back on those days, we had very little trouble in school and very little crime in the community. There were not many people in prison. In fact, there was only one prison in the whole state. It was at McAlester, for the really mean criminals. Because of the low crime rate we never had any reason to lock our doors at night or when we left the house. The town of Lindsay had only two law enforcement officers: the town marshal and one deputy on night duty. The deputy had very little to do. It was a lonely job and the jail was usually empty.

There were more honest, hard-working, reliable citizens that grew up in those days than any other time since. The crime rate has grown rapidly since they took the disciplining away from the parents and the schoolteachers. The prisons are all overcrowded, and they are building more prisons all over the state. I am so glad that my parents were strict with me. It made a better person of me, and prepared me for the things I needed to do to get along in life, especially when I was in the army. It made it easy for me to take orders and carry them out without question or resentment. After I grew up, I realized that my parents raised me right because they loved me. They never abused me, and they never punished me unless I did something wrong. We were a close family with love and respect for one another. None of us was ever arrested or spent any time in jail. I have always felt that if I ever had to go to jail, it would be the most devastating thing that could happen to me.

We all worked hard, which probably helped keep us out of trouble. There was always plenty of work to do on the farm. Dad started me off in the work force gradually. Seburn was doing the milking, and one evening he asked me if I would like to learn how to milk a cow. Well, I was always interested in a challenge, so I said "Yes". He showed me how to make the milk come out on an old red and white spotted cow named Pratt. She was named after Mr. Bob Pratt, the local cattle buyer and feeder

Bob Pratt

Dad had bought her from. From that day on, I was up at 5 o'clock every morning helping my brother milk the cows, feed the calves, and see that they had plenty of water. In the evenings, we milked the cows again and I turned the handle on the cream separator and gathered the eggs for Mom. Then in the spring, there was plenty of hoeing. Emogene and I would hoe the weeds and grass out of the cotton and corn while Scott, Seburn, and Dad were planting or plowing the rest of the crop.

Dad once brought home a homeless old fellow named Ben Dauraty to help us pick the cotton. Mr. Dauraty had no home or family, and he had not shaved, bathed, or washed his clothes for several days. He chewed tobacco and the tobacco stain was all over his chin whiskers, the front of his shirt, and both sleeves. I was disgusted with his condition even at my young age because my mom saw that we took a bath regularly and washed our hair, ears and necks. We bathed in a #3 wash tub with water heated in a teakettle on a wood-burning cook stove. Dad fixed a place for Mr. Dauraty to sleep in our garage, which was away from the house. He took his meals with us at the kitchen table. Up until I was five years old everyone called me by my middle name, Ben. But after Mr. Ben Duaraty left Scott and Seburn started teasing me about having the same name as him. I resented it so much that from then on I told everyone my name was "J.B." instead of Ben. I registered as "J.B." in school that fall, and all my records through high school had "J.B." on them. When I enlisted in the National Guard, however, I had to give my first name and middle initial. They asked what the "B" stood for because they wanted a middle name, too. But I didn't tell them. I always told them my middle initial only.

The very next year, Dad hired another drifter to help us pick the cotton. He was elderly also, but he took a bath, changed clothes, and washed his face and hands regularly. He was a very nice man. He called me Jake from the first time he saw me. I liked it all right. My family started calling me Jake, and my dad called me Jake from then on. A lot of people who knew me back then still call me Jake.

On the Bullock farm we had ten acres of prairie grass, which is now called 'blue stem'. We fed this hay to our animals in the winter for roughage. When I was five, my dad bought a horse-powered hay baler to bale the prairie grass. It was operated completely by our family and powered by our two mules Old Snip and Tiny. The hay was fed into the hopper from the top and then compressed into bales by a plunger coming in from the side and pushing against the hay. The plunger was about twenty feet long with a roller housing at one end. There were three large rollers in the box, and the mules turned the box by pulling a pole in a thirty-foot circle. The plunger went in and out three times for every full rotation. Scott brought the hay to the baler with a buck-rake pulled by two mules and he fed the hay into the hopper a pitchfork-load at a time. A guide bar led the mules and as they made their circle the three rollers would catch the end of the plunger and push it into the hopper, compressing the hay and pushing the bale through. Seburn would step down into the hopper to tromp the hay down after each plunge. When the rollers rolled off the end of the plunger a huge coil spring pulled the plunger back to starting position. The baler originally had wheels on it but Dad took them off so the baler sat flat on the ground and so the mules could step over the plunger as they made their circle.

My job was to keep the young mules going. Dad mounted a seat for me on the roller housing and it turned 'round and 'round all day. I would get so sleepy sitting on it that I could hardly keep my eyes open. I had a long horsewhip, but I did not use it on the unruly young mules. I just popped it now and then to keep them alert and to help myself stay awake. Mom's job was to punch the wires through and Dad would tie the wires and stack the bales as they were pushed out.

One day, Seburn was a little slow tromping the hay down into the hopper. The plunger closed in and he could not pull his feet out. Seburn cried out, and my dad immediately ran from the back of the baler and got in front of the mules. He grabbed the bridle bits and began to back them up. Luckily, the mules hadn't stepped over the plunger by the hopper so the plunger eased back out and Seburn was able to pull his legs out. He was not hurt except for being scared. I was so frightened that I sat motionless through the whole thing. If the mules had kept going, the plunger would have gone all the way in and broken both of Seburn's legs. If the mules had been on the backside of their circle, Dad would never have been able to get in front of them and stop them. I have never forgotten that day. I felt so helpless, and my dad reacted so quickly.

In 1930, my brother played on the Hughes basketball team with my Cousin Albert, Glen Bost, Truman DeVaughn, Leonard Bunch, Wes Duncan, and two or three others. They were a pretty good team for a little country high school. The coach decided to let them scrimmage against some of the previous year's graduates of Hughes just for practice. The graduate who was guarding my brother Scott was the same height as Scott but a little heavier and 6 years older. Scott was out-scoring him and out-guarding his defense, so the graduate got mad and started playing dirty. He was shoving and elbowing Scott under the basket and while running down the court. The referee let it get out of hand. The grad knocked the ball out of bounds so it became the school boys' ball. Scott went to get the ball to throw it back in bounds. Scott's opponent met him on the way back and shoved Scott up against the wall. Scott tried to step around him, but he elbowed Scott and shoved him up against the wall again. Scott dropped the ball and came out punching with both fists. Scott whipped him and knocked the guy down and out before anyone could get them to stop the fight. They called off the ball game.

A couple of weeks later, Scott's team was going to play Maysville High in a District game at Maysville, Oklahoma. My brother, Seburn, had heard at school that day that the tough guy was going to whip Scott at the Maysville game. When Dad heard about it, he decided to go to the game. He took Seburn and my older sister, Emogene, with him. Mom did not want to go so it was decided that I would stay at home with her.

We were still up when they came home that night. It was hard to tell who Dad and Scott were. Both of Scott's eyes were swollen shut. Both of his jaws were swollen out past his ears. Both of his knees were swollen twice the size they normally were. One of Dad's eyes was swollen. His jaw on that side was swollen so much you could not see his ear from the front.

Dad said that the 'tough-guy's' dad, his brother, four uncles, three brothers-in-law, and several grown cousins were at the game that night. They all left the gym two minutes before the game was over. Dad felt relieved because he thought they were going home. But it turned out that what they really did was go outside to get their eyes adjusted to the darkness and get their weapons out of their cars. Then they came back, stood at the gym door, and waited for the Hughes team to come out. The gym was separate from the school building and the team had dressed in the school building. There were no outside lights on the school grounds. When the ball team came out to go get dressed, the cowardly gang was waiting for Scott with tire tools, baseball bats, and 2x4s. The team was blinded since they were coming out of the lights into the darkness. Two guys grabbed Scott, threw him to the ground, and held him down while the 'Tough-guy' beat him in the face with a club and jumped up and down on his knees with his cowboy boots. The team went to Scott's rescue but they were pushed and shoved and knocked away. Their eyes were not accustomed to the dark either, and they all got black eyes and busted lips but nothing like what Scott and Dad got.

When Dad came out of the door, he and Emogene went to try to rescue Scott. They knocked Dad to his knees and began to kick him in the jaw. Emogene was yelling, "Leave my Daddy alone!" Seburn came out just behind Dad and Emogene and immediately got into the fight. He got his knife out and did a great deal of slashing. He cut some guys across their arms and faces, but the blade broke off in one guy's shoulder. Then he and Cousin Albert grabbed some discarded clubs and really started banging the tough guys around.

That seemed to be the turning point of the fight. Seburn said the cowards all left at the same time in a hurry. They got in their cars and drove away. Dad and Scott were 'laid-up', unable to do anything, for over a month. The rest of the basketball team was black and blue for several days.

The fight was never reported to the law enforcment officers. This happened over seventy years ago. In today's time there would have been an investigation. I am sure there would have been several indictments for assault and battery, assault to commit bodily harm, and assault with a deadly weapon, to name a few. My family moved on with their lives after that. I don't remember Dad or my brothers ever talking about it after their wounds healed. But it was really hard for me to forget and forgive like I was supposed to do according to the Bible. It was especially hard when I saw any of the cowardly family who were involved in the attack that night. As time went by I did my best not to dwell on it or even think about it. I can still remember how Dad and Scott looked when they came home. Even today I have a horrible feeling when I think about what they did to my Dad and brother.

Chapter 2
The High School Days

On January 1, 1931, soon after my tenth birthday, Dad rented a much better farm nearby. It was the Scott Moore farm just across the road, east of the Bullock place, where we had lived for the last nine years. The house was a quarter-mile farther east. It had five big, 16x16 foot rooms and a porch all the way across the front. In those days, all the farmhouses were box-type buildings. They did not have a double wall with sheet rock on the inside wall. The walls were 1x12s, and the cracks were covered with 1x4s. The floors were wood, and the house was hard to heat on cold nights in the winter. Dad would not leave the fire burning after we went to bed because he was afraid the house would catch on fire. But we had plenty of big, thick comforters that Mom had quilted to keep us warm.

This was a 200-acre farm, with 160 acres of good bottomland in cultivation. Forty acres were covered with timber, and we used that for pasture. There was also an eight-stall broomcorn shed and two of the finest water wells in the country. The water in both wells was cold and sweet. We could not lower the water level in either of them no matter how fast we tried to draw the water. The well by the back door of the house was a bored well with an eight-inch casing and a 4x36 inch water bucket and pulley. The one down by the barn was a dug well, four feet across each way. It was twenty-five feet to water in either well. The casing in the big well was 1x12s reinforced with 2x4s every 3 feet. It had a 5-gallon bucket with a pulley on it. We used it to water the live stock. We drew the water with a bucket and rope because no country houses had running water or indoors plumbing in the houses. Very few houses in town did either. What we did have was a big wood-burning heater and a cook stove. We also had an outhouse. That year, Dad bought Mom a Maytag washing machine with a hand-turned wringer and a little one-cylinder gasoline engine, which turned the dasher. We had to use it out in the yard, because the exhaust smoked. We kept it covered when it was not being used. I turned the crank on the wringer for Mom and kept the water hot in the wash pot and carried the hot water and poured it in the washing machine for her. We were all well pleased with the new method of washing clothes, especially Mom and Emogene because they did not have to scrub clothes on the rub board anymore. Right away, Dad built Mom a nice brooder house to raise her little chicks and turkeys in. A small kerosene stove heated it. He built another building for a blacksmith shop. He bought an anvil, a large vise, lots of hammers and tongs, and a forge for heating metal. From then on, he sharpened all his own plowshares, go-devil knives, lister points, and more.

Our neighbors on the farm just east of the Moore place were Mr. and Mrs. Neal Miller. They had four boys named Lester, Chancey (who were about Scott & Seburn's age), Charles, and Eddy (who were about my age), and three girls named Marie (who was about Emogene's age), Alta, and Aliene. To the north of them lived Mr. and Mrs. Cameron. They had sons named Paul and Tince. West of our place was Walter and Jack Rankin. Further south was Vernon and Turman DeVaughn. Across the road lived the Bates girls, Lois and Dorothy. Those two, the Miller girls, and my older sister Emogene were real close friends. They grew up together, went to school together, played basketball together and visited each other when they had spare time. West of the Bates place was J.B. and Kenneth Reynolds. After high school, J.B. married my sister Emogene. Farther west lived Mr. and Mrs. Bunch. They had nine boys and one girl, Bonnie. Four of the boys were older than Scott and had married and moved away. Leonard, Jack Donald (we called him "Square"), Grady, Cecil, and Rass ranged in age from Scott's age to younger than I was. Leonard and Jack Bunch married Lois and Dorothy Bates after they graduated from high school.

Although we all had to work hard we got a break once in a while. Sometimes we would go swimming in one of the nearby farm ponds. There was also a nice deep swimming hole in the Washita River on the Harry Moore farm about two miles north of our house.

The first Sunday after we moved in, all our neighbor friends came over and we played work-up baseball in a vacant field. Work-up baseball is played when you don't have enough men for two teams. When the batter is batted out he changes places with one of the fielders.

Our friend Square had a burro that he brought over sometimes. The burro was gentle to ride unless you rubbed him hard with a stick or corncob. That made him buck, and we took turns trying to ride Square's burro while making him buck. I never could stay on that burro. Square was the only one I can remember who did not get thrown off.

Once, we made a cable swing in a cottonwood tree in the

pasture. Scott climbed up to the top and pulled up a cable and clamped it around a huge limb. We tied an old tire at the bottom end about two feet off the ground and made a great swing just like Uncle Finley's. There was also a big elm tree close by. We would pull the tire up in the elm tree with a rope, someone would swing out, and when the swing came back, another person would jump on with the first person. I would always wait to be the third and last person to jump on. I would dive through the air and just barely be able to catch the cable just above the tire and hang on. Even at an early age I liked a challenge.

Sometimes we played a little game of jumping across a canyon. There was a canyon in our hillside pasture that ranged from six to ten feet wide and four to eight feet deep. The person who could jump across at the widest place was the winner. Each one could choose the place where they wanted to try to jump. If one succeeded, he could move to a wider place and try again, until they reached their limit, which was when they fell in. I did not do very well at jumping because I was one of the youngest boys in the group. All of them could out-jump me. Some of the older guys brought their horses and jumped on horseback. It was interesting to watch, but I never tried that. Seburn had a roan mare named Madge and, on her, he could jump across the widest place across the canyon. He started at the narrow part and gradually worked up to the widest. Dad gave me a mare named Old Kit, but I never tried to jump the canyon on her; she was over 20 years old when he gave her to me. She was his saddle horse before he and Mom got married.

In those days, we called a horse or a cow by their name, and we always said "old" before the name. I guess it was just the custom, or a habit that we picked up. We would say "old Spot" or "old Beck" or "old Tom" or "old Madge", or in the case of my horse, "old Kit." Old Kit was a beautiful dapple-grey. She was gentle and easy to ride. I took good care of her and always saw to it that she got plenty to eat. I rode her often to bring the cows into the lot. (These days lots are called corrals.) Sometimes when we were not working in the fields, I rode her around in the pasture, just for fun.

I also worked old Kit in the fields, pulling different one-horse plows such as the A-harrow, the double shovel, the one-row walking planter, or the Georgie stock. Sometimes I worked her with old Madge, Seburn's mare, to pull the go-devil.

Old Kit died when I was eleven years old, leaving me without a horse to ride. She was 25 years old when she died, an old age for a horse.

When I was 10 years old, Dad bought a beautiful purebred Hereford yearling bull from Mr. Bob Pratt, the cattle buyer who had sold us our red and white milk cow. This calf was so gentle that Dad led it home with only a lariat rope around its neck. He was so proud of that bull calf. We saw them walking in the road, coming toward the house, and we all met them just outside the yard gate. Dad was telling Mom how much he paid for the bull and how he would make a fine herd bull. Seburn said to me, "Jake, why don't you ride him?" We were behind Dad, and that was all the encouragement I needed. I hopped up on the bull's back. He let out a snort and a bellow and started bucking, right past Mom and Dad. Dad braced himself for the jerk he would get when the bull got to the end of the rope but they were so surprised that they didn't say anything.

Dad turned the calf and he kept bucking in a circle. I was hanging on until we got back about to where I had gotten on. Then the bull calf threw me high in the air and I fell on the hard ground. Seburn was doubled over laughing. He thought it was the funniest thing, but no one else was laughing. Dad walked away and led the bull to the feed lot. He never mentioned the bull ride to me, ever.

A couple of years later, that bull was grown and still really pretty. One day, we cut a field of oats for winter-feed right near the pasture. We took the fence down and hauled a load of the loose hay and stacked it in the corner of the pasture. The cows saw us and were so curious that they started toward the haystack. Dad left me behind to keep the cows out of the hay and he and my brothers went back to the meadow for another load of hay. He said we would put a fence around the stack later. The cows kept coming, and the bull was leading the way.

I waved my hands and shouted at the advancing herd. All of the cows stopped, looked, and turned back, but that old bull just kept coming. His head was lowered, bellowing like he was mad. I wasn't afraid of that bull, but I respected him and was not about to take him on, one on one. I retreated around the haystack. On the way I picked up my pitchfork, and as I came around the other side of the haystack, he was standing broadside to me, eating hay from it. I made a run at him with my pitchfork held high, like a javelin thrower. I let it fly as hard as I could, straight at the bull's side. It hit him just above the flank, behind the rib cage. In one motion, the bull kicked high with his left hind leg, over the pitchfork handle, and brought it down hard against the ground. The handle broke near the fork, but the pitchfork was buried so deep that it stayed in his side. Mister Bull wheeled and went away back to the herd.

The next morning at daylight, I walked from the house to the cow lot to milk the cows. I saw a huge white object down in the pasture, about 50 yards from the barn. It was too dark to tell what it was, so I walked down to take a closer look. The white was the bull's underbelly, and he was so bloated that two of his legs were sticking almost straight up. And then I realized that he was dead. I looked real close but did not see any blood. The bull was lying on his left side, the side where I had struck him with the fork. He had either lost the fork somewhere in the pasture, or he was lying on it. I went to the cow lot, and went about my chores, milking the cows. I was pretty worried. While I was milking, I saw Dad coming to the barn. My heart went up into my throat. He spied the strange white object and went down to take a look. When he came back by the cow lot, he said to me, "The bull is dead, he must have had a heart attack. I don't know anything else that could have killed him." I had mixed emotions. I felt guilty, and I was relieved. I never told him what happened, but I never did feel good about it. I kept that secret because I was afraid I would get a whipping, but that still did not make it right.

Seburn and I milked 5 or 6 cows every day all year long. We always had plenty of good, sweet milk to drink. I still like it to this day. We turned the cows into the pasture to graze during the day and kept the calves in the lot. It was just the opposite at night; the cows were kept in the pen and the calves were turned out. They always bedded down before morning, but never in the same place. Dad awoke me each morning at 4 a.m. and I went through the wooded pasture in the dark, until I found them and drove them to the lot, so we could milk the cows. We tried tying a bell on one, but it did not make sound while the calf was lying down. I did not have a flashlight.

One day when Seburn and I were walking through the pasture to gather some pecans, we came upon one of Dad's Hereford cows. She had just given birth to a baby calf. She was pretty wild, and when she saw us, she got real nervous. The closer I got, the more nervous the mother cow got. She began to stomp and turn around real fast. That should have warned me, but it didn't. She threw her head high into the air with her nose down, and suddenly she bawled, lowered her head and came after me. I had gotten real close. Too close to suit the mother cow. I turned and ran as fast as

I could run back toward my brother. I knew there was a fence not far from where he was. He must have known what would happen because he was already on the other side of the fence about 50 yards away. He was yelling, "Run, Jake! Run!" And run I did. By the time I got close to the fence, the cow was only a few feet behind me. I knew I could not jump the fence, but I did not slow down. I dove, head first, between the second and third barb wires without touching either wire. I remember looking up as I lay on the ground to see where the cow was. She had stopped up against the fence with her head high in the air, looking over the top wire at me. She was mad as could be, and her eyes showed that she meant business. My brother stood by, laughing so hard he could hardly stand up. The cow turned around and went back to her calf. It was hard to believe that I dove between those two wires without a scratch, but I hate to think what would have happened if I had not made it. When I asked Seburn why he did not warn me that it might be dangerous, he said, "I knew you could outrun her, Jake."

It was a blessing to have my older brothers. They taught me a lot of things: how to shoot a shotgun and a rifle, how to make friends and get along with other folks, how to swim and hunt, how to play baseball and basketball, how to play hard and do the best I could, how to be tough and how not to cry when I fell and hurt myself. They also taught me how to defend myself in a fight. In the winter, we hunted in the woods at night, and set traps. I ran the traps in the morning before breakfast. We caught opossums, skunks, and rabbits. We could sell a nice large opossum or skunk pelt for 25 or 30 cents at the produce store in town. I never forgot those times. They were good times, but they made me very conservative, and I still am. I try not to spend money foolishly.

My sister Sarah Emogene was two years older than I was. She was the only girl until my sister, Fannie Lou was born on September 12th, 1927 Emogene was the only girl until Fannie was born so she was very special to Dad. Mom had raised her to be a good little helper even while she was young. The night Fannie Lou was born, Emogene and the three of us boys were taken to stay all night at the Miller's house a half-mile east. We had never stayed at a friend's house overnight and had no idea why we were there. We played all night in the yard, in the field, and in the barn. Some time after midnight, all of us boys went to the Cameron's farm where their boys, Paul and Tince, were breaking some bottom land with their International Farm-All tractor. We rode the tractor and plow and played until daylight. When the sun came up Seburn suggested that we should go home to feed the livestock and milk the cows. When we arrived we were very surprised to find the new addition to our family, beautiful little Fannie Lou. It was just two and a half years later on February 3rd, 1930 that we were sent away to stay at the Miller's house again. When we came home that time my youngest sister, Lois Mae, was there and our family was complete.

My dad taught Emogene how to drive when she was 16 years old, and she got her driver's license. At that time, Dad owned a 1933 B Model Ford sedan. Dad had decided that it would be a good idea to mow our alfalfa at night. He and Scott were mowing the hay and Mom decided to send them a midnight snack. Emogene and I took it to them in the car, and I talked Emogene into letting me drive the car back to the house. When we got to the garage, I forgot to put on the brake in time, and the car ran into the back of the garage. The backside of the building came loose at the bottom, while the top held. The whole backside raised up and rested on the hood of the car. I was out there until 3 o'clock in the morning pushing the section back into place and nailing it. It looked real good when I was through with it. I'm not sure, but I don't think Dad ever knew about what I did to his garage that night. If he did notice, he never said anything about it.

The next summer, Dad began to let Emogene take the car to town on Saturday night to go see the late show at the Blue Moon Theater. But she always let me do the driving

An early photo of Main Street, Lindsay, Oklahoma

Saturday evenings were big days for us when we got to go to town. Everyone went to town on Saturday if they were not working. Dad drove the old Model T Ford truck, and Mom and Emogene rode in the cab with him, while we boys stood up on the back and held on to the cab. In town, Dad bought things he needed for repairs on the farm: tools, nails, staples, wire, etc. Mom would sell the cream, butter, and eggs we had saved that week and buy groceries, clothing, and other household supplies. I always helped Mom unload the cream and eggs at the produce store and carry the groceries to the wagon or the truck, whichever we had taken to town.

Afterwards, I sometimes walked all the way down the three blocks of Main Street, then crossed to the other side and walked back to the other end of town. Sometimes I would stop along the way and listen to the three local World War I veterans tell about their experiences during the battles of the Great War. They told how it was to fight in the mud, rain, and cold weather, about the dead and the dying, and the wounded. One of them was my uncle. Mom said that they stayed drunk all the time, and hardly ever worked, and their wives earned a few dollars doing washing, ironing, and housework for other folks. The men then spent some of that money on booze. I could not understand why they talked about those things; I thought that if they kept those memories to themselves, they would go away and soon be forgotten. Mom said they would not talk about it if they were not drunk. I did not have any money, but sometimes Mom gave me a dime for helping her with the groceries, and I would go to the western matinee at the Blue Moon or the Fox Theater.

I had some very good and very strict teachers from first grade

Lindsay's Blue Moon Theatre

Note 25¢ barber shop on the right.

through high school. As I said before, this was an age when teachers had the authority to make students do what they were told, and punish them if they refused. My first grade teacher was Miss Anna Howard. She started me off really well in school. She made it seem like fun. Miss Howard came to see Mom just before school started. She found out that I could recite the multiplication tables up to 12 times 12 and some poetry I had learned while Emogene and Seburn were learning it for school. She talked mom into starting me in school early, when I was five.

Miss Watkins was my second and third grade teacher. She was very strict, but she was a good teacher. When I joined the National Guard eleven years later, her brother Lieutenant Watkins would be my executive officer. He was a good soldier and a fine officer, and I was proud to serve under him.

Miss Marie Vaughn was my fourth and fifth grade teacher, and was also very good. She was a well-organized lady and knew how to get the most out of us. She kept advancing my learning and made it seem like fun. She married Mr. Forehand, a local Lindsay man, and they both retired in Lindsay.

My sixth grade teacher was Mr. Lloyd Garner. He was my first male teacher and he was strict and very good to us. He married Onetta Welch, a former student of Hughes High School. They continued to live in Lindsay after they retired.

Mrs. Gertrude Merritt was the strictest of them all. She taught me in seventh and eighth grade. She was Superintendent George Merritt's wife, pretty plain spoken, and she always meant what she said. She did not allow any horseplay or nonsense. She had pretty red hair, and when she talked, you listened to her. She could chew you out until you were ashamed of what you had done, but she was nice and kind to us when we did our assignments and did not horse around. She continued my learning and was one of the best teachers I ever had. We had a contest in her class to see who could memorize the most poetry. We had to recite the whole poem in front of the class without a mistake or a hesitation in order to get credit for it. I won the contest by memorizing over 1200 lines of poetry, and the prize was a book called _Real Dogs._ It was an interesting book and a treasured gift, and I kept it for a long time.

I got chewed out a few times in school, but not for anything that was serious. I never got a paddling or did anything bad; I was just mischievous. Mrs. Merritt had a pet saying that I had never heard before: "If the shoe fits, wear it." That one is still used a lot in these times. Another saying that I think she invented was "You can't have your cake and eat it too." I had never heard that before and I was a little amused by it. I wondered why anyone would have a piece of cake and not eat it. I remember the true meaning of the words finally soaked in.

I had some fine teachers in high school, Mrs. (Stephen) Cudd for English, Al Burris for Science, Mr. Russell for math, and Mr. King for Coach. My dad, mom, sisters, brothers and those fine teachers made me proud to be a God fearing, law abiding person, always considerate of other people, listening to their problems, and willing to help when needed. I am so thankful that they pointed me in the right direction.

Starting to school early made me the youngest student in my class every year until I graduated from high school. At that age, one year makes a lot of difference. I had very little in common with my classmates, but it did not bother me. I just did not have any close friends until I joined the National Guard after I started to college at the age of 17. I played baseball and basketball and made the team all four years in high school because I was big for my age and athletic. I made good grades every semester and had the second highest-grade average in my class. I was salutatorian and gave a speech at our graduation.

Hughes High School was a typical country school. A two-story brick building with each classroom heated in the wintertime by a big coal-burning stove. If you stood up close to it, you got one side too hot, while your backside was too cold. There was no air-conditioning; it had not been invented yet. Our gymnasium was an old wooden building across the schoolyard from the school building. The school building burned down during the summer after I finished eighth grade. We had classes in the gym, the teachers' quarters, and an old storage building, while the new building was being built.

In high school, we only took four subjects each semester. I had plenty of time during study halls to do my homework for the next day. I had been taught to use my time real well, and our study hall teachers, as well as all of our other teachers, made sure that there was no horseplay or idle students. In those days, the teachers were in charge of discipline in the classrooms and on the school grounds, and they could decide what the punishment would be for breaking the rules. There was no static from the parents, and I must say that it was very, very rare that anyone misbehaved. If the teacher did not

33

feel like doling out the punishment to a student, she would send him to the Superintendent. That usually happened when two boys lost their tempers and got into a fight. If they could not resolve their differences quickly, the "super" usually gave them a paddling. High school was more routine for me but I did have a couple of fights my sophomore year. Both fights were with seniors who were griping at me because I was getting more playing time at basketball and baseball than they were. Each time I told them to take it up with the coach, but that did not stop them. They started calling me names and even said I was afraid to fight them. Both fights were pretty evenly matched. We were about the same size, and both times we fought to a draw when the coach separated us. I was not very good friends with either one of them afterwards, but since the fights stopped the griping we got along okay. I did not believe in carrying a grudge because I believed it would waste that much of my life. I never really liked to fight, but I certainly was happy that I knew how to defend myself, especially once I got into the army.

I was six-feet, five inches tall and weighed 190 pounds by my sophomore year. Some of my classmates had failed to pass to the next grade two or three times, so some of them were two or three years older than me. Most of them married or were engaged by the time they graduated. Because I was so much younger than my classmates were, my two older brothers were my closest friends until I joined the National Guard. I was the only one in my class who went away to college after high school. Some of the kids who lived in town went to work in filling stations, restaurants, grocery stores, and drug stores, but the country boys had no place to live in town and no transportation. Some even quit school. The pay in the local stores was $10.00 to $12.00 a week for 10 to 12 hours a day, six days a week.

Most of the girls were ready to marry because that was the only way they could get away from home. Young couples would move into an old house and the husband would hire out as a farm hand because their parents did not have any money to send them to college. It was the only type of work available for them. The old fashioned fathers did not believe a teenage girl should leave home or live alone. Some of the girls who went to school in town lived at home after graduation and worked at local businesses. The girls in my class were interested in getting married to the older classmates but I did not care. Marriage was the last thing on my mind.

There were very few unwed mothers when I was growing up. The parents were so strict about their daughters going out with a boy. They knew the boy's family, were close neighbors, or knew the boy personally. They might also have a serious talk with the boy and discuss some strict rules. Very few of the young men had a car, but some used their dad's cars. There was an unwritten law back then, but it seldom had to be carried out. It was called the "Shotgun Wedding Law." If a guy got a girl pregnant, her father or brother (or both) would come after him with a shotgun and make him come with them and marry the girl.

My cousin, Albert Worley, was older than I was, and graduated from Hughes High School before I did. He still lived at home with his parents, Uncle Oscar and Aunt Bessie, near the Hughes School. He had not married or even gotten serious with a girl; he was real shy around girls. Albert bought a 1934 Ford Sedan. He and I liked the same things (rodeos, calf-roping, playing pool, and just riding around). He usually came and picked me up on Saturday nights and Sunday evenings. I liked Cousin Albert because he never got excited, and was always in a good mood. He was honest, and we always got along well. He did not drink alcohol or use tobacco. My senior year in high school, he moved away to Arizona and later got married to a real nice girl. When I talked to Albert about any kind of a situation that I questioned or didn't like, no matter how small it was, his favorite quip was, "You will never know the difference a hundred years from now." I never knew him to worry about anything. I learned a lot from Cousin Albert including how to be patient. After my saddle horse, old Kit, died, I did not have any means of transportation of my own, so I went to town on Saturday night either with Emogene, in our family car, or with Albert. On Sunday, Albert and I drove here and there in his car, but if I needed to go to the schoolhouse during the week, I had to walk. It was two miles to the school from our house. We did not have a regular period to practice basketball during school hours so during the fall and winter we had basketball practice two nights a week. I had to walk to practice which began not long after school started in the fall until basketball season was over after winter.

My time to roam through the wooded pasture shooting my cap pistol at imaginary targets was slowly coming to an end. My father

A One-Row Walking Planter

decided that I was old enough and strong enough to start tackling many of the jobs in the field, like hoeing cotton and corn; operating the one-row walking planter, the A-harrow, or the go-devil; picking cotton; gathering corn; baling hay; building and repairing fences; and many other things.

In my lifetime, there have been so many improvements in machinery and the way things are done on a farm. Now there are big tractors with cabs that can plant or plow six rows at a time.

Our first hay baler was the old horse-powered one. The next one was a stationary baler on wheels powered by a tractor on a belt. Then came the pick-up baler pulled along by a tractor. It had a pickup attachment in front that picked up the hay from a windrow. It only took four men to operate it: one to drive the tractor, one to punch the wires through, one to tie the wires, and one to stack the bales on a two-wheel dump trailer that was attached to the baler. Dad liked to own his machinery so he could do his baling and threshing when it needed to be done. He owned a hay baler, a broomcorn baler, and a broomcorn thresher or seeder as it was called. When he was not using the machines for his own crops, we did custom work for the neighbors. He charged a fee for the use of the machine plus our wages, and Dad was able to pay for the machinery and any repairs that were needed, and it gave him some extra income. Very few people in the neighborhood owned these types of machines.

Dad had three big healthy boys to help him operate his

Broomcorn Seeder

equipment. Scott and I usually operated the broomcorn seeder while Dad and Seburn ran the broomcorn baler. Mr. Earl Buford invented

36

a part for the pick-up hay baler that tied the bales mechanically. That device eliminated two hands from the crew: the person who punched the wire through and the one who tied it. Then along came the newest type of baler that rolls the hay into huge rolls out of the windrow. This makes feeding cattle really easy. You just set a roll of hay out in the pasture with a forklift and leave it until they eat it up.

We were poor in those days, but we didn't know we were poor because we had never had any extra money, nor did anyone else. But we had something better than money; we had love and respect for one another. My sisters, Emogene, Fannie, and Lois were precious to me, and my older brothers Scott and Seburn looked after me and taught me so much. They also expected me to carry my part of the workload and other responsibilities, such as chores and working in the field. I always felt good when I was assigned some particular job to do. It made me feel like they had confidence in me and trusted me to do the right thing. At this age, I needed very little motivation when my dad or brothers showed me how to do something and encouraged me. I would do my very best, and always tried to do it right. I took pride in learning to do new things; I liked responsibility, and loved to please those around me. I liked being able to do anything that anyone else would do. I loved being trusted with new jobs, and working for people who appreciated it.

The Washita River Valley, which runs from Chickasha through Alex, Bradley, Lindsay, Maysville, and Pauls Valley, Oklahoma is good farming land. Most of the good bottomland in the Washita River valley was planted with broomcorn in those days. The valley is 45 miles long from Chickasha to Pauls Valley. In some places, the valley is 5 or 10 miles wide, with hundreds of creek bottoms along the way. During the years from 1920 to 1950, the main money crop in that area was broomcorn, the stuff that straw brooms were made of before plastic was invented. Every farmer in the whole valley raised broomcorn. There were lots of huge warehouses by the railroad track. Back then it was the main source of income for farmers, but they don't raise it there anymore. Plastic brooms can be made less expensively and with much less labor. There are still a lot of reminders of broomcorn there, however. The old broomcorn sheds, for instance, are now used for other purposes: hay barns, carports, feed sheds for livestock, and more. Probably 75% of the farming land in that area at that time was planted in broomcorn each year. These days, those same fields now grow alfalfa, soybeans, and corn.

Farmers hauled their bales of broomcorn from all over the valley to Lindsay to sell it. Buyers were there, ready to make offers for the exact grade and type of broomcorn their manufacturers wanted.

Broomcorn Street - Early 1930's

The broomcorn marketplace for the entire area was Broomcorn Street in Lindsay, Oklahoma. There was a slogan back then: "Lindsay broomcorn sweeps the world." It was literally true. Most of the factories were up north in Ohio and Illinois, where many of the buyers lived. The broomcorn was also shipped to other parts of the world -wherever there was a place that wanted to make brooms.

Although the industry is now gone forever, the traditions will live on in the hearts and minds of those that lived around and worked in the broomcorn industry. Even though broomcorn is not raised there anymore, the old Broomcorn Street sign and some of the huge warehouses are still there, with the faded names of the buyers who once owned them still visible.

Scott Moore Broomcorn Warehouse, Lindsay, OK

The folks who were hired out to harvest broomcorn were called "Broomcorn Johnnies," except for the ladies who helped, and they were called "Sallies." I can't tell you why; they were named long before I was born. The early-bird farmers planted their broomcorn in late March or early April so they could harvest their crops first. The date they were shooting for was July 4th. Mr. Harry Moore was harvesting on the Fourth of July almost every year. Almost all the neighbor men and their sons would show up when a farmer was going to harvest his hay or broomcorn to try to get a job. Most of the neighbors were ready for the harvest to start. After a long winter and spring they needed the money. After a long period without spending money, they were ready for some grocery money. The Johnnies and Sallies came from far away, all over the state, and some brought their families and camped under the river bridge east of town. They cooked over an open campfire, and slept on the ground. They would come in wagons, some covered wagons, on horseback, in old Model T Ford cars, Model A Fords, Chevy trucks, and some even hitchhiked. There was a special knife for cutting broomcorn, called a Johnny Knife. It had a short, wide blade and a short round handle. They were sold in all the local stores. I have a couple of old Johnny knives in my storage shed to this day.

Chapter 3
Broomcorn

Broomcorn is sorghum. Planted in good soil, it would grow fast to a height of 12 to 15 feet tall. The head or straw was about 18 to 25 inches long. It would be ready to harvest about 10 to 15 days after the head began to emerge from the top of the stalk. The Johnnies would have to bend the stalks over so they could reach the heads to cut them off. There was a system of doing this where the Johnnies walked down the row grabbing stalks in two rows at a time, bending them down, crossing them behind their backs and making a table out of the stalks. This process served two purposes: to make the Johnnies able to reach the heads to cut them off and to make a place to pile the heads after they were cut off the stalks. When the heads were cut they were placed in piles on every other table, while the off-tables made a space for the broomcorn float. The broomcorn

A Load of Broomcorn-Going to the Shed

float was a special wagon that would drive between the two tables that had the piles of broomcorn on them. The haulers would load the float with broomcorn and haul it to the broomcorn shed.

Late in the evening, the crew was called out of the field and they went to the shed to thresh what had been hauled in that day. It took a couple of hours to thresh, but even if it took until after dark, we stayed until it was all threshed and in the shed. If it was piled up with the seed overnight, it would naturally heat up and start to mold. That would damage the straw and it would have to be sold at a lesser price. To keep that from happening, the broomcorn was spread out on slats in the broomcorn shed to dry for about 10 days. Then it could be baled into 400-pound bales.

All of it was hard work. When I first started working in the broomcorn, wages were fifteen cents an hour and the noon meal was furnished by the landowner. The wife, with the help of several of the neighbor women, would cook enough for the crew. A crew was about 40 men. A regular day was 10 hours, from seven in the morning until six at night, with an hour off for lunch. There was no overtime

A broomcorn threshing crew

pay for over eight hours or on Saturdays or Sundays; overtime had not been thought of then. If anyone slacked off, they would be fired immediately with no bonus, no severance pay, no anything but wages due at that time. There were always more than enough hands that came in the morning to try to be hired, and some would stay around to see if anyone was fired. Several of the farmers would plant broomcorn early so they could be the first to harvest, but they could not fool Mother Nature. Every year I can remember, the harvest started on July 4th. It lasted until a few days after the first frost.

In 1931, wages went to twenty cents an hour and the hands brought their own lunch. My brothers and I were not paid when we worked for Dad, nor did we expect pay. We received lots more than money – three meals a day, a roof over our heads, clothes to wear, a paid education, and a whole lot of love.

My first job in the broomcorn was water boy (or "water jack," as it was called). Dad made a rack on a two-wheeled cart pulled by two horses. He placed a wooden 55-gallon barrel in the rack. I had to draw water from the well and fill the barrel with cool, fresh water, and water the Johnnies at both ends of the field and in the middle, if the rows were very long. I was a very popular boy on a hot day. After I started doing this for Dad, a neighbor, Mr. Milt Devaughn liked the idea and hired me to water his Johnnies. He paid me the wages of a hand: twenty cents an hour for the rig, the team, and me. For the next two years, I water jacked for several neighbors around the country. I earned enough money to buy my school clothes, books, and had a little spending money. But that did not last. Dad decided that he needed me to help Scott operate the broomcorn seeder. When we were not threshing for Dad or for a neighbor, we would hire out to cut broomcorn for a neighbor. I had no trouble getting a job in the harvest when I was not working for my dad. Dad taught me to be honest, work hard, and do a good job. My brothers and I were bigger than anyone our age, strong, and tough. We tried to be the fastest and best hands in the crew. I always had a good feeling when I was asked to do special jobs that only took one person to do. I took pride in doing them well. We always worked hard and did a good job wherever we hired out and all the farmers knew who worked hard and who did not.

It took the entire crew to thresh up after a days cutting. Scott and I took the seeder to the shed and set everything in place and the crew came in time to thresh. Some of them carried the corn from the loaded

My brother Seburn with a broomcorn baler and bale

wagons to the table, and others cut the heads into small bunches and butted the stems even. They passed the bunch to Scott or me, since our job was to feed the seeder. We spread it out onto belts where a special chain clamped the heads and carried them into the seeder.

The heads were moved between two spinning cylinders that had spikes on them. The cylinders knocked the seed off the heads and a large fan blew the seed out the back of the seeder into a pile. Another group of men, sometimes women, would carry the seedless heads into the broomcorn shed. We called them "ants" because that's what they looked like. They would pick up a load and carry it into the shed, drop it off and go back to pick up another load over and over again, just like ants. Inside the shed a person we called the "shelver" spread it on slats to cure and dry.

Broomcorn Drying in the Shed

The seed pile out back was long and narrow and sometimes huge depending on how much broomcorn the farmer had to harvest. The seed would go through its natural heating stage for a few days and turn into sweet silage, which was good to feed livestock in the

Broomcorn butting table, seed pile and shed

winter for roughage. They spread the remainder of the silage on the fields to rebuild the soil. After about 10 days of curing, the baler and a few good men and women came and baled the broomcorn into big bales that averaged 400 pounds. Dad and Seburn ran the baler for the public and Scott and I ran the seeder.

The weather was always hot and dry and the fuzz off of the broomcorn was knocked off by the baler and the seeder. This fuzz would fog the air and was very uncomfortable because it irritated the eyes and skin, especially when a person was hot and sweaty. The workers all wore long sleeve shirts and buttoned up their sleeves and collars to try to keep the fuzz out. Some wore bandanas or scarves around their necks or over their face.

After a long day of working in the broomcorn or hay, or plowing in the field, my brothers and I were hot, dusty & sweaty. After dark we would go down to the big well by the barn, fill a #3 washtub with cold water, and take turns drawing a 5-gallon bucket of water and pouring it on each other while standing on the well cover. It was a good way to cool off while washing away the dust, fuzz and sweat. One time the rope broke and I had to climb down in that well to recover the bucket.

One Saturday I was cutting stalks in a field near the road to town. I was using a two-row stalk cutter pulled by three horses. At about noon, Dad told me that he was taking the rest of my family into town but that I was to stay home and finish cutting the stalks in that field so he could start plowing it on Monday. I wanted to go to town so bad that I almost cried when all of the family came by in the old Model T Ford truck. Dad, Mom, and Emogene were all in the cab, while Scott and Seburn were standing up on the truck bed, holding on to

the cab. They waved as they went by, and I got so depressed that I started feeling sorry for myself. For the first time in my entire life that I could remember, my dad was mistreating me and favoring the other kids.

It took all evening to finish cutting the stalks in that field and my family had come back by then. I rode the stalk cutter to the barn, then unhitched, unharnessed, and fed the team. Then I went about doing my chores, milking the cows and gathering the eggs as if everything was all right with me. By the time we had finished eating supper, it was dark. I went outside and walked down to the barn and on toward the wooded pasture. I had no idea where I was going but Dad's little rat terrier named Trixie followed me. While I was walking through the pasture in the dark, I decided that I would run away from home. As I remember that night, I believe I was trying to show my dad that I was unhappy, and that he could not treat me that way anymore. But young people should know that running away is not a very good way to handle that situation. If I could do it over, I would talk it out and not keep my feelings inside.

All the clothes I took were what I was wearing. I did not know where I was going or what I would do when I got there, or what I would do for food.

I walked through the woods into the fields toward the river. Harry Moore's house was between the highway and the river. It was two miles from our house. I had traveled this way many times each summer to swim in the river. There was a deep hole behind Mr. Moore's barn where the river made a sharp turn. I was very familiar with the water depth and current.

When I reached the river, I took off my shoes and carried them and Trixie across in waist-deep water above the deep swimming hole. The other side of the river was low-bottom, heavy in trees, with thick underbrush and driftwood. I picked my way through with little Trixie staying close to my heels. It was a lot darker in the woods than it was coming through the fields.

Sometime around midnight, I began to get tired, and I sat down on a log to rest. I was so tired that I didn't want to go any further. I was also hungry and thirsty.

A storm cloud had been gathering in the northwest. I could see lightening flashing and could tell that it was getting closer real fast. Suddenly, the wind started blowing real strong. It was howling in the treetops, swaying them back and forth. My pants were still wet from wading the river. I started to feel the cold, and started shivering. Little Trixie was shaking and whining, so I slid off the log to lie down on the ground. Trixie snuggled up against me. As I lay there, I began to think about what I had done. I had left a loving, caring family and was stranded in the middle of the woods where I had never been before, hungry, tired, sleepy, cold, and miserable, with nowhere to lie but on the ground. I had two choices. One was to work my way through the underbrush to the foothills in the north (I had no idea how far it would be), and turn west on the dirt road that led to Lindsay, and then take the south road out of town that led to Great-Grandpa Evans' farm. I bet he would let me stay with him, and I could help him with his chores and his farming. I could milk the cows, feed his pretty dapple-gray horses, and play checkers with Uncle Elb. Besides, Grandpa had the first radio I ever saw in my life. We had visited them many times before Grandma died, and I remember sitting outside in the dark after supper, listening to Amos n' Andy on his radio. My other choice was to get up and go back home and take my lumps.

While I lay there daydreaming, watching the treetops sway in the wind, it kept getting colder and colder. It began to look like it was going to rain any minute. I realized it was about 10 miles to Grandpa's house, after I got out of the wilderness. And I was so tired.

I stood up and decided that the best thing for me to do was go home. After all, home was not so bad; I always had plenty to eat and a soft, dry bed to sleep on. And I had a family that cared for me. Home would beat lying out there in the woods, hungry and cold, and about to be rained on. Dad and Mom had always taken good care of me. So what if I did not get to go to town. I could go next time. Maybe Dad did need the stalks cut and depended on me to do the job for him. What would he think of me if I left home because he asked me to do a small job for him? What would Mom and my brothers and sisters think? Was I going to try to please my father, who had worked hard all his life to take care of his family, and take on the duties and responsibilities that he laid on me? Or was I going to cop out and run away when I did not like the assignment that he gave me? Both my brothers had told me, "Nobody likes a quitter."

After that little talk with myself, I started picking my way back through the underbrush the way that I had come, with little Trixie following close at my heels. I waded the river carrying the dog and my shoes, crossed the highway, and went through our fields and the wooded pasture. As I walked, I thought about what I would tell Dad in the morning. I finally decided that I would just tell him the truth. I know now, with all my heart, that I made the right decision. But I soon realized that I would not have to wait until morning to tell him. I could see a light shining through the kitchen window. It was 4 a.m. when I opened the door and walked in. Dad was leaning against the kitchen wall in a straight-backed chair, wide-awake. "Where have you been?" he asked. "I was worried about you." I told him I was angry because I had to work and the other kids got to go to town, so I ran away from home. He asked me how far I got, and I told him I got across the river into the swampland, that I got tired and the wind started to blow and a cloud came up, and I decided to come back home. He said, "I'm glad you came back. Let's get to bed and get some sleep; it will be time to get up real soon." He went to his bed and I went to mine and he never mentioned that night to me again, nor did I mention it to him. I never left home again until I went away to college at the University of Central Oklahoma in Edmond, Oklahoma.

After that night, I realized what a good family I had and how blessed I was to be a part of it. I never think of those times as being bad times. Now I believe those early years with my family gave me confidence and made me a better person. Also, when I started felling sorry for myself, all I had to do was look around, and I could find someone who was much worse off than me. Mrs. George Merritt, my seventh and eighth grade teacher, would have said, "Don't cry over spilled milk."

When I got in bed I suddenly remembered that Dad once told us that he had run away from home when he was 12 years old. He never went back until his dad died many years later. His mother died when he was 10. His dad married a woman with 5 children of her own. Dad said that she was mean to him and his brother Oscar and sisters, Vineybell, Corene, and Alma. She would make them wait until she fed her own children, and then they could have what was left. She made them do all the chores while her children played. She only did this while their father was away from home, and when they tried to tell their father, he would not believe them. He scolded and shamed them and took their stepmother's word instead of theirs. When there was quarreling and fighting among the children, the step-mother would separate them and whip my dad, his brother (my Uncle Oscar), and their three sisters, but would do nothing to her own children. Dad and Uncle Oscar both left home. I went to sleep that night thinking that my dad probably understood more than he let on about my leaving home. But I also realized that he had a far better reason to leave his home than I did.

Farming was done with horse-drawn equipment until about 1934. There were a few tractors around that were used to power stationary threshing machines by using a wide belt on the pulley. But there were no tractors equipped to do row crop planting and cultivating. The year that farm tractors went on the market, all the farmers in the valley sold their horses and mules and bought a tractor. There were John Deere, International, Allis-Chalmers, Minneapolis Moline, and Case. The handy little Ford tractor did not come out until in the forties. When it came out, Dad sold all his horses and mules except one team of big black mules, a big bay mare named Bell, and a small sorrel mule named Snip.

Old Snip was born to Seburn's mare, old Madge. Dad had made a pet out of her from when she was a colt. She was the prettiest mule I ever saw. She was light red, and her mane and tail were red, too. Her nose was white all the way up to her eyes. She was feisty and ready to go all the time. She took quick little short steps and she loved to run and kick up her heels when she was out in the pasture where there was plenty of room. She tossed her nose high in the air and to one side as she walked.

Scott and Lois with Old Snip giving Dad a kiss

Dad taught old Snip to come to him and nuzzle his cheek with her nose. He called her by name and when she came, he told her to give him a kiss. He always rewarded her with a handful of grain or sugar. Dad said many times that he wished old Snip was broken to ride so he could ride her down to the pasture to see about the cows, or through the community when he took the school census in the winter, but Dad was not a bronco buster, so he never tried to ride her.

I was no bronco buster, either, but I had ridden a few calves and the yearling Hereford bull Dad brought home a few years earlier.

47

One Sunday afternoon, I stayed at home alone while Dad and Mom and all three of my sisters went to visit Grandpa and Grandma Diggs. Soon after they left, I went to the horse lot, bridled and saddled old Snip, and led her out to a plowed field near the barn, As soon as I mounted her she looked back at me sort of wild, turned her ears back, lowered her head, and started bucking. She bucked like a rodeo bronco. She turned this way and that, crow-hopped, kicked her hind feet high in the air, and every two or three jumps she let out a mournful bray. She bucked all the way to the road that led to the barn, and then just quit and trotted down to the lot gate. Somehow I managed to stay on her for the whole ride. When she stopped I got off and petted her and rubbed her for awhile, until she got her breath, and then I mounted her again. This time she did not buck at all. I rode her around for about 30 minutes and taught her to rein this way and that when I needed to turn. Then I unsaddled her and fed her some oats and rubbed her down again.

When I was young, if I did something that I did not think my dad would approve of, I would sometimes not tell him about it. This was one of those things. I did not tell Dad that I rode old Snip. It was not that I thought he would punish me, but because I was afraid he would tell me not to ride her anymore. Years later I would regret that I did not tell him, or anyone else in my family, about that day.

During the next four years of high school, when we had basketball practice at night or any other activity at night, such as class parties, I would ride old Snip to the schoolhouse. I always waited until I had finished doing my chores and had supper with my family. I would tell them where I was going and go out the front door like I normally would. Then I would walk around the house to the barn, saddle old Snip, and off we would go.

One night after basketball practice, someone suggested that we have a horse race. There were about ten boys riding horses and I was on the mule. It was dark, but there was a full moon and we could see real well. We lined up across the road, and someone yelled, "Go!" We were off and running on the hard clay dirt road. We must have sounded like a herd of buffalo. By the time we had gone about 200 yards, I was in second place and gaining on the little mare just ahead of me. We had come up to a farmhouse on the side of the road and a big dog came charging out, barking loud and mean. The little mare in front of me went right by the dog, but the dog kept running straight at Old Snip's head. I thought my mule would fade to the left to run from the dog, so I leaned that way, but instead, she cut sharp to the right to go behind the dog, and I fell off of old Snip and on top of the dog. Fortunately, the dog broke my fall, and I was not hurt. But the dog was hurt and scared so bad that he went back to the house howling. Old Snip stopped close by and waited for me.

In Texas, the wheat began maturing and was ready for harvest in May and early June. This is where the combines started harvesting. They would move north as the weather warmed up and the grain ripened. By August the harvest had moved through Oklahoma into Kansas and southern Nebraska.

About the middle of August of the year I graduated from high school, Ray and Lindsay Williams, Doug Arnold and myself just sort of dared each other and decided to go on the wheat harvest which was moving north. We hitchhiked first to Oklahoma City to Ray and Lindsay's sister's house. She fed us the last good meal we would eat for the next several days and drove us to Edmond, Oklahoma, about 20 miles north of Oklahoma City. There we decided to catch the first north-bound train that stopped. It was a passenger train. None of us had ever ridden a train before or even been inside of one. The train stopped for only a minute to pick up a passenger. We were hiding behind a hedgerow that ran along beside the track. When the train started to move, we ran and crawled into the only space, the steps to the coach. The conductor had closed the door and the metal piece that covers the steps. Two of us got into the steps at the same door. There was only room for one person in each set of steps. There was no place to go any farther. I thought there was a crawl space behind the steps that we could get in. We did not have enough room to turn around. Our knees were on the bottom step. Our feet and legs stuck out past the side of the train. I could see out of the corner of my eye that we had already gotten up to speed. The telephone poles were whizzing by our feet really fast. We could do nothing but ride all the way on our knees to Guthery which was about twenty miles.

We got off as soon as the train stopped and disappeared into the crowd. We each bought a candy bar and a Coke. That was our supper. About sundown, a freight train came from the south and slowed down as it approached the station. We caught on to the box cars. My brother had ridden freight trains to California and back the summer after he graduated from high school. It was the fad back then for young boys to ride freights to California and back just for the thrill of it. He had told me that he had been told never to catch onto a freight car on the back end. Always catch the front of the boxcar. The momentum could throw you in between the cars, break your grip and cause you to fall down in between the cars only to be run over. At the time he told this I had no idea that I would ever ride on a freight train. We waited until the train started speeding up. I pulled myself up on the first step and when I glanced back I saw Lindsay run hard into the metal stand that signals the engineer which track he is on. He recovered quickly and caught the next car. We rode the train all night. After dark, we rode on some tank cars near the rear of the train. Later in the night, we found some empty refrigerator cars. We opened the top door and climbed down into one of them. We tried to sleep but no one was able to. We arrived in Kansas City's rail yard about daylight. There was another train station on the north side of town with tracks leading to all points north. We walked through the city to the north railroad station. That would take us to where the wheat was being harvested at that time. They were switching boxcars from different tracks. We rested in the shade and went to sleep while they made up the train.

As the train began to move out of the yard, we slipped to the north track where the train was headed. We thought no one saw us. We hid in some weeds by the right of way. When the train began to pick up speed, it gave a highball whistle, a toot-toot. We came out of our hiding place and ran along-side the train but quickly came to a sudden halt. There, in front of us, stood this big tall 'Bull'. That is what railroad policemen were called. He was the biggest, meanest looking man I had ever seen. He held a long-barreled 'hog-leg' pistol in his hand. He was waving it back and forth in our direction. He told us to stand still and not move. We stood there as he told us to do until all of the cars and caboose had gone by. Then he told us to turn around and run through the yard and never come back. He said if he ever saw us around there again that he would use that pistol on us. We turned and ran and did not stop until we got across and out of the railroad yard.

We then decided to go back through town to the south train station. They were making up a train there that was heading out on a west track about sundown. It was made up of all boxcars and the doors were all open. We ran along beside the cars, jumped up, and managed to lift ourselves up into the doorway. This was another new experience for us. Two of us got into the same car and the train was picking up speed. I went and stood in the door and stuck my head out to make sure the other two guys got in a car behind us. While I was looking out the open door, the engineer locked the brakes. I guess he was stopping to let the brakeman catch on to the caboose. The metal door slid forward so fast I could not get my head out of the way fast enough or stop the door from slamming. The door caught me just in front of my ear and slammed my head against the door jamb. I somehow shoved the door open and staggered back inside and fell down. The train then started up again and we were on our way out of Kansas City.

That was the most miserable night I had ever spent in my life. My head hurt so bad I could hardly stand it. I lay on the floor of the boxcar all night. I could not sleep. By morning I had a high fever. I passed out I guess becase I got so hot from the fever. My buddy woke me the next evening and told me we had to get off because they were side-tracking the empty boxcars. I managed to scoot to the door and get out. We walked to the edge of the yard and sat down in the shade. One of the guys bought some candy, soda pops, and some old bread but I did not eat. My head was throbbing and my jaw had swollen out even with the edge of my ear. I think we were in Wellington, Kansas.

In a little while, a passenger train came through headed south and we caught it. This time we grabbed onto the steel bar by the door and swung in between the cars. The only trouble was that the engineer saw us get on. In a few minutes he opened the door and told us to come inside. He was very kind and polite to us. There was no one else in the car. He seated us at the rear of the car and went up to the front of the train. Everyone but me began to smile and say how this was "all right". I would have smiled but I hurt too badly. We cruised along for a couple of hours then the train slowed down and stopped. The conductor came back and said "End of the line! Everybody out." When the fourth one of us stepped on the ground, the train began to roll and the conductor closed the door and watched us through the glass.

When we looked around we saw only three buildings. There was a small train station, a small grocery store, and a filling station. All three were closed and locked and there was no one around. I bet that conductor is still laughing. He had put us off in the middle of nowhere. There was a Sunday newspaper in a rack in front of the store. When we saw the date on the paper we realized that we had been away from home for a week. There was no one in that little town. There were no houses there either. We walked all the way to Enid, Oklahoma. The next day we caught a freight train to El Reno, then another to Oklahoma City, and we hitchhiked back to Lindsay.

In the end, I learned a well-remembered lesson. I had been gone a week and a half and was seriously injured, had very little to eat, and did not have a bath or change of clothes since I had left home. I had wasted the entire week and a half and had gained absolutely nothing for taking that trip. I was glad to be home and my folks were glad to see me. My mother worried about me because my face was still swollen, but I was all right in a couple of weeks, just in time to go off to college.

The Worleys
Seburn, Blanche, Jack, Scott, and John,
Lois & Fannie in front

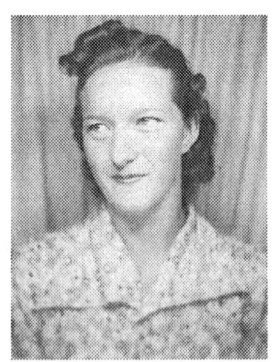

Chapter 4
College and the National Guard

After my graduation from high school, my science teacher, Mr. Al Burris, encouraged me to go to college at the University of Central Oklahoma in Edmond, Oklahoma. My brother Seburn offered to loan me the money if I wanted go. I told him I would like to go very much and I saved all the money I made working in the broomcorn that summer. Seburn and Mr. Burris were good friends and on

University of Central Oklahoma

September 1, 1939, Seburn drove me to Edmond (about 90 miles north of Lindsay) where we met Mr. Burris at his parents' home. After lunch we went to enroll and we toured the campus. While I enrolled at the college, Seburn established an account for me at the bank in Edmond. I took the required courses of English, history, algebra and health. For my physical education courses I took basketball and since I had always liked to swim I took swimming.

We returned home and the next day I packed my suitcase and Dad took me back to Edmond. I was 17 years old, weighed 190 pounds, and all that I owned fit into a suitcase. I moved into an upstairs room near the campus with Allen Price, who was also from Lindsay. The owners lived downstairs and were very nice.

The next few weeks I ate a lot of day-old bread and peanut butter and jelly sandwiches. We could buy a loaf of day-old bread at the bakery for five cents. A few clothes, books, and the enrolling fee took all of my summer wages, plus, I had to write a check for some of it. It bothered me a lot that I was now officially in debt to Seburn. I knew that I would pay him back some day; but I did not have the slightest idea when that would be.

For the first time that I could remember, I had so much idle time on my hands that I did not know what to do. Gene Stine, one of my classmates from Alex, Oklahoma, had gotten a job at the Weaver Hotel just west of Main Street. He said there were 25 oilfield workers who stayed there. They served two meals a day and each man took a lunch to work each day. Gene Stine said he waited tables and that they were going to hire someone else to help in the kitchen to wash dishes. I applied for the job that day and was hired. The owners were Mr. and Mrs. Weaver. They were elderly, probably in their sixties. The pay was room and board. Just what I needed to get through the year. Gene and I shared a room near the kitchen.

Mrs. Weaver ran the hotel. She did all the cooking and washing and ironed the sheets and pillowcases. She worked hard all day, every day, while Mr. Weaver left after breakfast to play dominoes at the pool hall all day. They were real nice people. She woke Gene and me at 4 o'clock every morning and we started helping her prepare breakfast. Gene set the table while I made toast and helped Mrs. Weaver make the sandwiches for the men's lunches. I also helped her by handling the hot pans out of the oven or peeling potatoes in the evening and vacuuming the hotel on Saturday. I had to vacuum the dining area, the stairs, the hallways, and all 25 rooms. My main job, though, was washing dishes. Mrs. Weaver was surprised that I did not mind working. As soon as Gene brought the first dishes from the table I started washing. I learned how to wash dishes while I was growing up. I was always finished with the chores in time to go to my 8 o'clock class. Mrs. Weaver was nice to work for and I was thankful to have the job. I did not want to spend any more of Seburn's money than I needed.

Right after I started working at the hotel, another classmate told me about the National Guard. He said the armory was only five blocks south of the campus. They spent two hours in uniform every Wednesday night and they received one dollar for those two hours. I worked every summer in the hot sun for 20 cents an hour, so I thought it was a pretty good deal. The very next Wednesday night I went down to the armory. This was Regimental Headquarters Company, 179th Infantry, 45th Division. I went into the office at the command post and was greeted by the clerk. I told him I would like to join. He referred me to the company commander, Captain Messina B. Murray. Captain Murray was the eldest son of Governor Bill Murray. One Saturday evening, while I was still in high school, I heard Bill Murray speak from a truck bed in front of the Blue Moon Theater in Lindsay while he was campaigning for governor. He was a fast talker and used a lot of "cuss" words. They did not seem to belong in his speech to me. That night Dad said one of the men he was standing by made a little rhyme:

"God made man,
And he made him in a hurry.
He had a little left,
And he made Bill Murray."

Bill Murray's son, Captain Murray, was very nice and immediately put me at ease. Within a few minutes he had asked all about me, my family, where I was from, what I was doing, what I was studying to be, and why I wanted to join the National Guard. I was very frank with him. He told the clerk to give me an application, and I signed up. The only problem was I was only 17 years old. I wrote down 1920 instead of 1921 for my birth year because I wanted to join so badly. I thought that no one would ever know. After all it was only two months until I would be 18 years old.

Captain Murray had a way with people that made them feel good about themselves and proud to be in his company and proud to be ready to serve their country. He seldom ever chewed any one out. When he did it, was in a private place where no one else could hear. He never chewed me out; however, there were a few times I felt like I had it coming. He never raised his voice to anyone on the parade ground on the drill field. I consider myself very fortunate to have been able to serve under such a noble man and an expert soldier, particularly during my rookie years. Captain Murray's side arm was a sword. He handled it expertly. When he took charge of the company from the 1st sergeant for reveille, retreat, or close order drill, he would go through all the sword routines such as salute, present arms, orders, and so forth. He was a master swordsman and I enjoyed seeing him perform the drills.

I quickly began to look forward to Wednesday nights. Mrs. Weaver had no problem excusing me in time to walk down to the armory. On the third Wednesday night after I joined, Captain Murray announced that we would drill two nights a week, starting immediately, on Wednesday and Thursday nights. I was looking forward to it. I would now earn two dollars per week. The very next Wednesday night Captain Murray announced that the company would go to camp in December. He had already spoken to the college president. We would be excused that week and would be able to make up what we missed.

He told us that the reason for stepping up the program was that Washington and the high military command were a little uneasy about what was going on in Europe at that time. Hitler was making many threats to Poland, France, and all the Balkan countries. He was also arresting all the Jewish men in Germany, young and old, and putting them in concentration camps. Word got around that Hitler intended to take over those countries by military force, a prediction that came to pass real soon.

We continued our drills on Wednesday and Thursday nights. There was a lot to learn. First, I learned that the executive officer, Lieutenant Watkins, was the brother to my second grade teacher at Hughes. Lieutenant Watkins was also a good soldier. Like Captain Murray he was a patient officer and took the time to get acquainted with everyone. I liked these two men more than any other officers in the army. They were my idols, the soldiers I wanted to be like, and I was proud to be under the leadership of these two great men.

Sergeant George Jacobson was also a good soldier and my friend. He called me 'Twirley'. He had been in the guards a long time, so I asked him if he could tell me some things that had happened to him in the guards. He told me that soon after Governor Bill Murray was elected, the roughnecks went on strike at an oil well site on the capital grounds in Oklahoma City. They formed a picket line at the entrance to the location. They armed themselves with big wrenches and threatened anyone who crossed the picket line and Governor Murray called out the National Guard. Since the Edmond armory was only 15 miles away, they got the first call. His first sergeant called out about twenty men, got them in uniform, issued them 1903 World War I rifles without ammunition, loaded them into 1½ ton trucks, and headed for the capitol building. When they arrived, there were a dozen roughnecks lined up on the street leading to the location. The army truck parked across the street from them. The sergeant went through the routine army commands in a loud voice, "Unload; fall in; dress; right dress; at ease." About that time the roughnecks started walking toward the soldiers with their wrenches drawn shouting threats and calling names. Then, without hesitation, the sergeant yelled out, "Load rifles!" Every soldier jerked back the bolt on his rifle and slammed it shut in unison as if they were loading a shell into the chamber. It made a loud noise. Then he ordered "Take aim!" Every man raised his rifle to his shoulder and aimed it at the approaching men. The roughnecks stopped, made an about-face, and ran for cover behind some pipe racks. They did not show up again the rest of the day. Another unit relieved Sergeant

Jacobson's squad that afternoon and they returned to the Edmond armory, laughing all the way about the big bluff they had pulled with no ammunition. The strike was settled in a few days. The sergeant in charge of the squad was an older man and retired, so I never got to meet him, but he was still remembered by the older fellows in my company.

There were many interesting challenges in the National Guard. Regimental Headquarters Company was responsible for communication to all three battalion headquarters companies and to all twelve rifle companies as well as back to division headquarters. We had a twenty-four drop field switchboard powered by a generator with dozens of big rolls of double strand insulated telephone wire, plenty of field telephones, and tools to cut and splice the wire and hook up the phones and switchboard. Our routine on Wednesday and Thursday included classes on how to hook up the instruments and how to operate the switchboard. The army had certain shortcuts, special ways, to do everything and it had to be done that way. It was all new to me, but it was not too hard to learn. We also did close order drill in the big gym-sized room of the armory. We were issued rifles, but no ammunition. We learned the manual of arms, different formations, how to keep in step, and rifle inspection. Our uniforms were heavy, woolen, army-green, World War I style, pegged-leg breeches, wrap-around leggings, and the old, straight-brimmed, dark brown Mountie-type hats. They did not have anything else and that is how unprepared our military was in 1939. We were also issued a wide, sand-brown belt with a big brass buckle and a blouse with four brass buttons for dress uniform.

When I told Mrs. Weaver about the extra drill night on Thursdays and the one-week maneuver in December, she was very understanding. She also let me off the next weekend and I went home to visit my folks. It was my first time home since school had started. I hitchhiked all the way, even through Oklahoma City. There was a restaurant on Reno Street in downtown Oklahoma City that had home-cooked meals for 25 cents. I always stopped there when I hitchhiked home, going and coming. Assaults by hitchhikers were very rare in those days and everyone stopped to give a serviceman a ride. I never had to wait very long for a ride. The way these times are, it's no longer safe to stop and pick up hitchhikers or even to help someone stalled on the highway.

It was great to go home and see the family. Since Dad had no one to help him farm the Moore's place, he moved to a smaller place near Hughes High School. He had more pasture land for his cattle and less farming land. I felt a little guilty about that, like I had let my folks down by going away to college. They did not seem to mind and it was too late to change that now. I only had a weekend pass.

On Saturday, Dad asked me if I would drive into town and buy some supplies for him. That sounded like it would be fun. He made me a list of the things he needed. I went out and got in the car and headed for town. I was halfway to town when I heard some giggling coming from the back seat. I stopped the car and turned to look under a small tarp that was on the floorboard. To my surprise, there were my two little sisters hid under the tarp. Fannie was 7 years old now and Lois was five. They had heard Dad and me talking about going to town and had gone out to hide in the car to sneak a ride. When I found them, I immediately turned around and headed back toward home. I admit I was a little bit anxious. I could almost see Dad and Mom running down to the creek, going up and back, looking for them, calling out their names. I worried all that time for nothing. They had not missed the girls when I got home with them. Dad was out at the barn working and thought they were in the house with Mom, and Mom thought they were at the barn with Dad. All is well that ends well. We all had a good laugh, and I went on my way back to town. I took the tarp out of the car and made sure I did not have any passengers that trip. I was so thankful that they were not missed before I got home with them.

The next week we were called to duty. We donned our uniforms, packed our barracks bags, and were loaded onto a troop train at the Edmond train station. They took us to McAlister, Oklahoma. We loaded on trucks that took us up in the mountains. It was government land and no one lived up there. We pitched our eight-man tents in straight rows facing a long company street. We put up the officers' tents, the supply tent, and the mess tent, and unloaded the supplies. By that time, we were all tuckered out and after chow went to our tents, made our bunks, and went to bed. We did not have cots for this maneuver so we made one big pallet. Each man kept one blanket to roll up in and we all fell asleep. We had no stoves either. The chow that week was good and there was plenty of it. Sergeant George Jacobson was a good mess sergeant. He would always shout, "There will be seconds!" and I always took

Mess Sergeant George Jacobson

him up on that. The food was bland but full of vitamins. It was not up to the standard of Mom's or Mrs. Weaver's cooking but it was close. It was a fun time for me that week. I knew all the guys in my tent, but we had time to get more acquainted. Our tent commander was Sergeant Dee Gregory. He was a good soldier, pleasant and good humored. He was an Indian and a senior at the University of Central Oklahoma. I still remember some of his philosophy. He said that the last time the United States Army had winter camp, they went to war shortly thereafter. Then he said we had nothing to worry about because we were in Headquarters Company, a non-combat outfit. Also, unlike the rifle companies, we would be far behind the front lines in a safe place if we did go to war.

I was glad to hear that because a couple of Mom's brothers-in-law and three other guys who lived in Lindsay had fought in France during World War I. All five of them became town drunks after the war. Always unemployed, they hung out at the pool hall or sat on the curb at the corner of Main Street and told stories about their days in combat. Their wives managed to make a living for them, taking in washing and ironing and doing house cleaning for the public. I suppose the men took part of the money to buy booze. I was skeptical of their stories at first, and I promised myself that I would never burden anyone with stories like that if I ever fought in a war and that I would never resort to drinking alcohol to drown my sorrows. Drunken people disgusted me. They lose their dignity and self respect, lower their moral values, and only want to make love or fight. Two of the old veterans died of respiratory ailments that year. Mom told me that they were in an area where the Germans used poison gas on them. All five of them were wounded in battle.

Once when I was at home, I stopped and listened to the remaining three tell about the horrors of war: the hand-to-hand combat, the constant shelling by the German artillery, the threat of poison gas, the wounded, the dead and dying, the cold rainy winters, and the muddy, soggy trenches. At that time, I still believed that if we keep painful things inside and never talk about them they will go away. It would take me over fifty years before I would find out that's not true.

We had a pleasant week in the hills of eastern Oklahoma. It was cold at night but we had no rain. I learned a lot of useful things. The hardest work we did was erecting the tents, unloading supplies, then breaking camp and loading the equipment. The two things that impressed me most were the statements my sergeant made that we would probably go to war and that, when we did, our company would be a safe place to be.

After returning to Edmond, we quickly got back into our routines and I turned in my make-up work. The professors in college were so different from my high school teachers. They seemed to distance themselves from the students. I guess that was from seeing so many students come and go over the years that they did not want to make friends with any one student. The second semester went by fast. In one of my classes, we were seated alphabetically. A young lady seated next to me was Judy Williams. When she found out I was in the National Guard, she told me she was dating a soldier in the Guards named John Juby. John was halfback on the football team and a real good soldier. He later became one of my best friends.

I made passing grades that year but not as good as I had made in high school. At the end of the second semester, I had written checks on the account my brother had set up for me for a total of $120.00 to cover my tuition, books, and supplies. I had worked for my room and board and had used my army pay for spending money. A year of college costs a bit more than that now.

Captain Murray gave me a leave of absence from the guard for the next two months to go home and help my Dad on the farm. I had to be back on the first day of August to go to summer camp. We would be going to Louisiana for three weeks instead of the usual two weeks because of the unrest in Europe. Hitler was overrunning the Balkan States and France was also one of his targets.

My Dad had more work than he could do. I was welcomed to the workforce. I cultivated the cotton, corn, and broomcorn. The red and white paint horse that Scott rode while he was at home and Dad's little mule with the white nose were my team for the summer. Old Snip and Shorty were all the work stock he had left.

We harvested Dad's broomcorn in July and I returned in time to get into uniform and leave with the company for Louisiana.

We camped near Pitkin, a small town eight miles from the Texas border in the tall pines.

I drew K.P. for the entire first week. We pitched eight-man tents before we retired to our bunks. We had cots to sleep on this time. The next morning the mess sergeant shined a flashlight in my face at 4 o'clock and told me my day had begun. I raised up and swung my feet off of the cot and to my surprise water was almost up to the bottom of my cot. It had rained the entire night and we had pitched our tent in a low place. I waded to the kitchen and helped prepare breakfast for the company. Afterwards I helped move our tent and my belongings to higher ground. Then it was back to the mess tent to wash pots and pans and peel potatoes.

It rained every day, two or three times a day. I decided that I was lucky to be working on K.P. in the mess tent rather than wading in the mud and rain out in the forest with the rest of the men. At the end of the week my K.P. duty was over and I joined the company in the field. I learned a lot about army communications during the next two weeks. We set up radios and talked to all the headquarters' units. We set up the switchboard and ran phone lines to all the company command posts and talked to them.

On the train going back to Edmond, we stopped for a few minutes in Tyler, Texas. My sergeant got off of the train and bought a newspaper. He came running back to the train shouting and waving the paper. He was yelling, "We are going to mobilize!" There it was in big, bold headlines covering the whole front page: "THE 45th INFANTRY DIVISION TO BE INDUCTED INTO THE REGULAR ARMY SEPTEMBER 20th." When we mustered out at the Edmond Armory the next day, Captain Murray told us to go home, be with our families, get our business in order, and report back to the armory September 20th and be ready for regular army duty. That was the end of my college career.

Chapter 5
Fort Sill – The Regular Army

We reported for duty at the Edmond Armory September 20, 1940, and were confined there for two weeks, receiving and checking supplies that we had not needed before. We had a few new recruits, and a half-dozen men took hardship discharges to help their parents make a living. That was allowed if the parents signed a paper that stated they were really needed at home. It never crossed my mind to try to get out of the army. I was comfortable so far with the army routine, I was a little bit curious to see what army life would be like, and I had made many good friends. I also knew in my own mind that Dad and Mom would do just fine without me. And I certainly would never have asked my parents to sign a paper for me to be discharged unless it was an emergency. Two weeks later we moved to Ft. Sill, Oklahoma. Civilian workers had built wood frames for our tents, which were west of the army barracks. We called it Tent City.

Tent City 1941-Compton, Danean, Joe Booth & the author, ready for duty

We had close order drill on the parade grounds every day. Each Saturday morning we had tent inspection by the company officers and 1st Sergeant, George Jacobson. There were eight men per tent and a non-commissioned officer, or "non-com," in charge of each tent. This time each man had a cot and a footlocker. Bunk beds had to be well made for each inspection. Footlockers had to be open with clean underwear and socks showing. The mess kit, canteen, silverware, and brass had to be shined and displayed in the foot locker tray.

We were all nervous on Friday night before our first inspection. We did not want anything to go wrong. Everyone in our tent stayed up almost all night shining mess kits, silverware, and brass. About midnight we decided to go to the P.X. and have a snack. As we walked along, I was talking to the guy next to me when a big guy from the artillery, about my size and weight, threw his shoulder and elbow into me and spun me around. I did not see him coming. By the way he looked at me, he had done it on purpose. He got real nasty about it and proceeded to dress me down, telling me to watch where I was going. Then he started loudly cussing me and calling me names while his buddies egged him on and encouraged him. I suddenly remembered what my brother Scott had taught me: surprise your opponent; beat him to the punch. Without a word I moved in on him and threw three rapid punches to his jaws. He went down and out. His buddies got real quiet. When I saw that he could not get up, I turned and walked away and we continued on our way to the P.X. I never saw that guy again.

As we passed our mess tent on the way back, someone suggested we break in and get something to eat. We raised the tent flapping and crawled in. The very first thing we saw was a stalk of bananas. Instead of taking a few each, we took the whole stalk and carried it to our tent. At reveille the next morning, the remainder of that stalk lay in the middle of the tent floor. Too late to dispose of it, we had to do something with it before inspection time. My good buddies decided that I was the least likely to be suspected. So we put the rest of the bananas in my footlocker under the tray. The inspection began. The officers entered our tent and walked slowly by each footlocker without word or touching anything as we stood at attention. My bunk was next to the last one. When Captain Murray came to my foot locker, he stopped and sort of unconcerned, as if talking to himself, he said "What do you have in the bottom of your foot locker, Private Worley?" I froze. I had several thoughts and all of them began with "why." Why did I let them put those bananas in my footlocker? Why did he choose to only look in the bottom of only my footlocker and no one else's? Captain Murray raised the tray of my foot locker and said, "Ah, bananas, eh?' He replaced the tray and walked out of the tent followed by the rest of the inspection crew. Everyone was shocked. I thought I was in big trouble, but I never heard another word about the bananas.

We had regimental inspection on the parade grounds in dress uniform once a week. The entire regiment would march out onto the parade grounds in companies. Our regimental commander, Colonel Gibbins, inspected each company. Afterward we passed in review. Before our first parade and review, 1st Sergeant Jacobson sent word for me to report to the C.P. tent. He told me that Captain Murray wanted me to be the standard bearer (to carry the flag) because I was the tallest private in the company. He told me to march in front of the company, two steps behind Captain Murray and one step to his right. When we reached the inspection area, I was to run ahead, come to attention with the flag, and the captain would march the company up even with me and line up on the flag. All twelve of the other companies would line up even with the flag to our right. That was fine with me. I felt honored to be chosen to carry the colors. There was not enough time to tell me anything else. I took the flag and got in place and the captain marched us toward the parade grounds in columns of fours.

Colonel Roarck had stationed himself at the edge of the parade grounds to see that the companies were in the right order, that everyone was in the proper uniform, and all that sort of things. As I came even with the colonel, he halted our company with a loud bellowing voice that was heard to the last company. The whole regiment came to a halt. He boomed out, "Don't you know how to salute an officer with the flag!?" I said, "No, sir." He kept chewing me out while the regiment listened while standing at attention. He even asked me how long I had been in the army. It was a shock to my ego. I had never been humiliated like that before. It is tough when you have to take something like that. Everyone knew to whom he was talking. For the next few weeks, I was teased by all my friends as well as by guys in other companies that I did not even know. Everything else went well on the parade ground and the inspection. On the way back I wondered if the captain thought I had let him down. Would I get another chance?

After we were dismissed and back at the company, Sergeant Jacobson asked me to come to the C.P. tent. He gave me a copy of "Army Regulations" and told me to study the procedure on how to handle the flag. That was all that was said. From then on I had the highest regard for Sergeant Jacobson and Captain Murray for giving me another chance to carry the flag and prove that I could do it. I learned the hard way that the army was not all bad like Colonel Roarck.

After that happened the United States Flag began to mean something special to me; a sacred feeling I've kept all these years. It hurts me when someone is disrespectful of the flag. I honor our flag as a symbol of what this great country means to me, and as a reminder of those who fought to keep it that way, especially those who died in battle, were lost at sea or were prisoners of war. If those who are disrespectful of our flag do not like what America offers them, maybe they should go to some other country and live. I'm really sure that they would quickly learn that the United States is by far the best country in the whole world. Patriotism is the element in our hearts and minds that makes us want to do our very best for our great and wonderful country when we are called on to do so. During World War II, almost everyone was patriotic and did what they were asked to do or at least everything that they were able to do. Since then some folks have not been willing to serve their country. I pity them because they do not feel proud to be an American.

Nothing boosted my morale more than being assigned a special, one of a kind position. I felt that Captain Messina B. Murray and 1st Sergeant George Jacobson had put their confidence in me and that I would do my best not to let them down.

The next few weeks, army life was very good to me. Captain Murray promoted me to Corporal. Sergeant Jacobson assigned me to a new tent to be tent corporal over seven new recruits who had just been assigned to our company. I soon learned that I had my work cut out for me. They had all been drafted. None of them wanted to be in the army. Three of them had just gotten out of jail. The other four of them were members of gangs in Oklahoma City. I had their respect during the day, but after retreat, they could go anywhere on the post until 11p.m. bed check. I told them if they were not in the tent at bed check I would turn them in as AWOL.

One of them went AWOL and was picked up in Oklahoma City on grand larceny charges. I never got him back. Within six weeks the other six were in the brig on the post. Two of them were arrested while stealing gasoline from the motor pool after dark. It seemed they were carrying the gas to their four buddies who were waiting in a stolen automobile that belonged to an officer. The four panicked and drove away. They were arrested while trying to drive out of the main gate without a pass. My batting average as a tent corporal was double zero. I never heard from any of them again. And it was just as well. They were nothing like any of the other soldiers in our company and they would never have fit in. So much for that!

Captain Murray had received an order from Regimental Headquarters to assign someone to inspect all of the kitchens and latrines in each of the thirteen companies each weekday. Since I did not have anyone in my tent, he sent for me and gave that responsibility to me. He told me that I was the inspector and that I was to write it up like I saw it, whether good or bad. I could inspect the kitchens and latrines in all thirteen companies in the morning, make my report, and return to my company in the afternoon in whatever training program we were doing. I liked the inspection duties. I got acquainted with new people in every company. I let every mess sergeant and 1st sergeant know the list of regulations that I had been given and that if I found anything wrong, I would have to write it in my report. They all accepted the challenge and they assigned latrine orderlies to clean the latrines each day. Right away I saw a great improvement in the cleanliness and neatness in every kitchen and latrine. I liked the responsibility and got along well with the sergeants.

The other good news was we began to get weekend passes. A lot of the swingers went into Lawton or Wichita Falls. I never went to town. Every time I went on a pass from Fort Sill, I hitchhiked home and spent time with the family. One time when I was home, I paid Seburn the $120.00 that he loaned me to go to college the year before. I had been saving my army pay, except for five dollars per month for toothpaste and shaving cream, just to pay him back his money. It was a good feeling!

After I paid my debt, I continued to save my pay. The army furnished everything I needed. It was a habit with me to make my money go as far as possible.

Another time when I was home on a weekend pass, my dad had broken his false teeth plate. Mom told me he did not have the money to pick up his new plates. He had been on a soup and soft food diet for several weeks. I had enough extra cash to pay for his new teeth. It was a blessing to see how happy it made him. My army pay had made it possible. It made me feel so very good to do such a small favor for Dad who had sacrificed so much for me while I was growing up. After that, I allotted all of my paycheck but $10.00 per month to my Dad so he could put it in a savings account for me.

Chapter 6
Camp Barkley-Near Abilene, Texas

The following March, we were moved to another new camp which was another tent city. Camp Barkley was nine miles southwest of Abilene, Texas, on the San Angelo highway. As our convoy passed through Abilene that day the streets were lined with people cheering and waving to us. That was my first time for that type of welcome. It sure was nice of the people of Abilene. Camp Barkley would be our home for the next year.

We immediately started 25 to 35 mile hikes down the highway west of camp, toward San Angelo. Just three miles from the main gate was the start of rolling hills. The first hill was a long, steep grade that made us all get real quiet and concentrate on breathing. That hill was also the beginning of a huge goat ranch called Hankins Ranch. The army signed a contract with Mr. Hankins to use his entire ranch for maneuvers. In exchange, the army would buy goat meat from him. We ate goat meat every day for the next year. Our mess sergeant soon learned to cook the meat so that it tasted pretty good, and it's a good thing, or else we were all going to go hungry at mealtime. We spent many nights camped out in those hills. We walked down the highway for 10 or 15 miles with full field pack, turned in at one of the gates, pitched pup tents among the little cedar trees, and slept on the ground. During the day, we had war games and practiced setting up telephone and radio communications between the companies and battalions.

I became good friends with three other young soldiers in the company because we had several things in common. None of us drank alcohol, we did not like to be around anyone who did, and none of us smoked tobacco. Drugs were very rarely used back then. I wish with all my heart they had never been brought into this country. Drugs and alcohol have ruined so many lives, caused so much sorrow and pain, and caused so many deaths and property destruction. But that is another story and I must add, a sad one.

The first of my three friends was Sergeant John Levi Juby was from Sperry, Oklahoma. He would say "Sperry is nine miles from Tulsa, downhill and shady all the way". He was a lot of fun. He was a full-blooded Native American Indian. He told us that his Indian name was "Benny Way B. Cigar". John loved to kid around, was rarely serious, was always in a good humor, and was very thoughtful. He was also a good soldier. He nicknamed me 'Tree-Top'. John played halfback on the University of Central Oklahoma football team the

year before we were mobilized. John was the only one of us four who had a girlfriend. She was Judy Williams, the girl I sat beside in class who told me that John was her boyfriend. While we were at Camp Barkley, John got a "Dear John" letter from Judy. That is what we called it when a girl broke off an engagement with a soldier. The break-up really hurt John but he was a survivor and kept his feelings to himself.

John Levy Juby 1917-1944

The second soldier in our foursome was Corporal Wayne Pittsenberger from Edmond, Oklahoma. Later he was promoted to platoon sergeant. He was also a fine soldier, calm, reliable, and pleasant to be around. He was levelheaded and good-natured and loved "the blues". His favorite vocalists were Lena Horne and Cab Calloway. He had a real good voice and could sound like and imitate Cab Calloway to a tee. If he had a girlfriend, he never mentioned her to us.

Sgt. Wayne Pittsenberger

The third man in our group was Sergeant William B. "Bill" Wier. He took Sergeant Jacobson's place as 1st sergeant when 1st Sergeant George Jacobson was promoted to master sergeant. When Sergeant Jacobson was promoted I was moved into the radio and telephone equipment tent with him to help him with inventory, equipment repair, and so on. I bunked with him for the remainder of our stay at Camp Barkley. Sergeant

Cpl. Max Thompson
1st Sgt. William Wier

Wier was a fine soldier. He was sincere, quiet, and good humored, and I soon learned that he and I also had a lot in common. He didn't like alcohol or enjoy being with someone who was drunk either.

We both liked sports, and he did not have a girlfriend and did not care to look for one. Bill liked to play golf. One Saturday afternoon Bill, John Juby, Wayne Pittsenberger, and I went to a golf course in Abilene and played golf. I had never played before but they were good instructors. After that day we played golf every time we had an opportunity.

All four of us shared the same ambitions; the same achievement goals, the same ideas and we always got along well together. We sometimes went to football games together at Hardin-Simmons University or to a movie either on the base or in Abilene on weekend afternoons. We usually had a steak afterward. We were in town seeing a movie one Sunday afternoon on December 7, 1941 when we heard that the Japanese had bombed Pearl Harbor. I was certain that day that the 45th division would soon go to war somewhere.

I had several fights in Abilene but never started any of them. It would happen the same way every time. We would be in a restaurant eating on Sunday night, waiting for the last bus to camp and some soldier would come in who had been drinking too much and say he could "whip the biggest guy in the house." Each time someone close to our table would say, "Here he is!" and point to me.

Liquor seems to give each person a different attitude. Some get happy, some get quiet, and some get mean. It seems to me that drunks always do things that they would never ever do while they were sober. The first time this happened to me, I tried to talk the guy out of it. I told him that I did not want to fight him. The more I talked the more he thought that I was afraid of him. It built up his ego so he started calling me names, like coward, among some curse words. I quickly decided that the best way to deal with this drunk was to meet him head on and beat him to the punch. So I got up and punched him out. His buddies carried him outside.

One Saturday night, a medic that I knew from our battalion came into the restaurant where my buddies and I were eating and he was drunk. He walked in and challenged the biggest man in the house. Someone pointed to me, of course, and he came over to our table and repeated his challenge. I tried to reason with him because I knew him and he knew me. He ignored everything I said and began to get loud, threatening and cursing me like all of the others had, and then he attacked me while I was still sitting down. I recovered and beat him up real bad. We met later that same week at camp while I was inspecting his company's kitchen. He looked terrible. He had cuts and bruises all over his face. He told me he was very sorry he did what he did and did not know why he did it. He asked me to accept his apology and I did. Then I walked away, puzzled why someone would do that to himself. I have never come up with the answer to that one. I guess I led too sheltered of a life when I was growing up to understand. I never felt proud of myself after any of these fights. Neither, however, did I feel like letting some guy beat me up for no other reason than just being present and pointed to as the biggest guy in the house. I never really liked to fight, but I was proud that my two older brothers taught me how to defend myself. The medic was the only guy that I ever saw again after we fought and he was the only guy that ever apologized for making me beat him up.

One day, Colonel Gibbons' chauffeur-orderly took a leave of absence. Captain Murray assigned me to take his place until he returned. It was a very pleasant assignment. The duty turned out to be driving the command car from reveille until retreat, five days a week. I liked for my superior officers to give me special assignments. This was another job that I had never done before. Sometimes the colonel would send me to deliver some papers to some other officer in the division. Sometimes I delivered papers to division headquarters. Later in the morning, I would drive the colonel to some type of meeting with another officer or group of officers. I would stand by with the command car for short meetings or the colonel would tell me to pick him up at a certain time.

After lunch I usually drove him into Abilene. He went shopping or met with the press or city or county officials. Colonel Gibbons was very pleasant and good at giving instructions. I enjoyed driving for him and talking to him those two weeks. I missed that job when it was over. I went back to my regular duties at my company, but not for long.

"B" Company was from Ponca City, Oklahoma. All of the enlisted men were Native American Indians. "B" Company was short several non-commissioned officers. One week after driving the command car for the colonel, I received another special assignment. 1st Sergeant Jacobson told me to report to "B" Company each day after breakfast to help train troops. I would return to my regular company each night.

I reported to the captain of "B" Company that morning and he assigned me to a platoon as a squad leader. My squad consisted of twelve Indian lads. I always got along with Indians. I have a little Indian blood in me from my mother's side of the family. My good buddy, John Juby, was a full-blooded Indian. My first squad leader back in Oklahoma was an Indian. The color of a man's skin never made any difference with me. What was in his heart and character was what counted. When the captain assembled the company, he marched us to the parade grounds for a little close order drill, which gave me a chance to begin getting acquainted with the troops. I believe that the officers were probably testing me to see if I would be good for the job. I must have passed their inspection: they kept me.

Each weekday morning for the next six weeks, I reported to "B" Company for duty. We marched out the main gate and about 5 miles into the hills, to one of the commando courses the army had built for our training. My company had never been out there. Only the rifle companies used them. The first one was used for a body-building course. There were walls to climb over, ditches to jump, tubes to crawl through, and hurdles to jump. My squad was surprised that I did all the exercises with them. And they told me so. One of them told me that they thought I would stand around, direct traffic, and yell at them. That first day was an icebreaker for me. I gained their confidence. From that day forward they trusted me. I took the lead and went through all the exercises first. That is the way I was. I never asked anyone to do anything that I did not do first. I liked to lead instead of send.

Later that afternoon during a break, the squad got in a huddle and was whispering and laughing. When I asked them what was so funny, one of them said they had nicknamed me "Long John". I thought that was neat. From then on I knew I had made friends with my squad. The platoon sergeant was also an Indian and he was a really good soldier. I wish I could remember his name. He also liked the name 'Long John' and always called me that. He chuckled a little because I took it in such a good-natured way even though the squad had thought of it.

One of the courses we used was about 100 yards square. It had several holes about the size of a foxhole and about waist deep. We were warned not to go in the holes. They each contained a stick of TNT with a wire running from each hole to the observation platform. Each one could be set off as we made our way through the course. The explosions were supposed to simulate artillery shells exploding in our area. The ground had been plowed and several tank-truck loads of water had been dumped on the entire field. It was a muddy mess. Two 50-caliber machine guns were set up to crossfire just a few feet above the field while we were crossing it.

They told us to crawl across the field on our bellies from one end to the other, not to stand up or crawl into one of the holes where the explosives were. The machine guns fired rapid fire and the TNT exploded as we crawled. This was only a 'make-believe' of what the real war would be like.

Another commando course was set up in a huge area covered with large cedar trees. There they had man-sized figures cut out of plywood with figures of soldiers in uniforms painted on them. These poster boards were placed every few yards throughout the area, three to five figures on each board. The boards were lying down with hinges on the front side and small wires attached to the top. When the wires were pulled from the observation platform the board with the soldiers drawn on it stood up and represented an ambush. We were supposed to shoot all targets until they fell backward. We were graded on how long it took to shoot down all the targets, how many shots were fired, the location of the holes in the targets, and how quickly the first shot was fired. When we shot down all targets on the board, we moved on to the next one.

My squad made a grade of "Excellent" that day. I was so proud of them; however, I could not take credit for their score. These guys learned to shoot somewhere else before I met them. Because I was worried about their safety, we had a short safety meeting before we went into the woods. I told them how important it was to keep abreast of the man to their right and all the other safety tips I could remember to help them keep from having an accident. It turned out they were a very careful group of young men.

After we completed all of the commando courses, we acted out some field tactics for different situations: how to keep in touch with each other, with other squads, with other companies on our right or left, and how to keep from firing on our own troops.

We then spent a week on the rifle range. All of the men in my squad made "Expert Marksman". Each one received an expert rifleman lapel emblem to wear on their dress uniform. Again I was proud of them. After that week I returned to duty in my own company with much satisfaction. I had made a lot of new friends. I had two months of infantry rifle training – something that no one else in my company had. The next day Sergeant Jacobson informed me that I was promoted to sergeant.

While we were stationed at Camp Barkley, I began attending

church at the chapel every Sunday morning that I was in camp. I had been neglecting to go to worship service. Deep down it had bothered me. I was the only Protestant that attended in a group of about a dozen men. The Chaplain always excused me just before they had communion.

I became a Christian when I was nine years old. My parents influenced me and taught me right from wrong. My mother read the Bible a lot when I was a small boy. I loved those old stories in the Old Testament, but later I favored the New Testament. They say you never forget your upbringing and that certainly was true in my case. I can still remember my Dad saying, "Everyone has a guardian angel." I believe that with all my heart. It gave me much comfort and a feeling of security all of my life, but especially when I was overseas during World War II and in a dangerous situation.

By this time I had really become adjusted to the army life. I even had thoughts of making a career of the army. I would have a long time to make that decision.

Chapter 7
War Maneuvers In Louisiana

In June, the 45th division was moved to Louisiana by truck. The highway we took to Louisiana ran through Decatur, Texas and right by the home of my Dad's sister, Aunt Vineybell, and her husband, my namesake, Uncle Ben. I wrote a note that said, "I will see you tomorrow," and signed and dated it. I put the note in a bottle and, when our convoy went by their house, threw it in their yard. I always did like to surprise someone, or do something on the spur of the moment. That was a little maverick in me.

This was a shuttle movement, so we were unloaded in a large pasture near McKinney, Texas. We pitched camp and stayed there two days, while the trucks returned to Camp Barkley to bring another group to McKinney.

My friend, Lee Brown, and I hitchhiked to Decatur the next morning. We went to my aunt and uncle's house and had a good visit. We had lunch and a big piece of homemade apple pie. Decatur is special to me because it was there that I had become a Christian just 11 years before that visit. At that time, I was not totally aware of my responsibilities in being a Christian. I knew it had changed my life, my attitude, and my outlook on life, family, and friends. Little did I know that in a few months I would learn how great God is; and how wonderful it was to be able to turn to Him in prayer when I had a spiritual need.

We returned to our outdoor camp in the pasture that afternoon. The next day, my friends, Sergeant George Jacobson, Sergeant Bill Weir, Sergeant John Juby, Corporal Wayne Pittsenberger, and I rented a boat and went fishing in Lake Dallas.

The next morning we loaded into the trucks, and continued on our way to Louisiana. We camped in the woods near Camp Polk, and prepared to begin our war games against the 36th Division from Brownwood, Texas.

My two brothers and I were allergic to poison ivy all our lives, and each one of us had several cases during our lifetime. Within a couple of weeks I broke out all over my body with poison ivy. I spent the next three weeks in the hospital at Fort Hood. When I was released from the hospital they transported me along with several other soldiers, to our main base, Camp Barkley, instead of taking me back to my company in Louisiana. Though I kept my rank as Sergeant I was assigned to the stockade as Corporal of the Guard of one shift of the guard. There were 3 shifts; we were on 8 hours and off 16 hours. That is as close to being in the brig as I ever want to be. I was to wake up the guards before their shift to be certain they were dressed and on duty, and make sure that none of the guards went to sleep on their shift. That was the most boring thing I had ever done in my life.

At the end of the second week things had not gotten any better, so I asked for and received two week's furlough. Instead of going home this time, I hitchhiked to Pharr, Texas, way down on the Rio Grande. I had folks there, all immigrants from Oklahoma. They had grown up on the farm and were tired of farming, but jobs were scarce in Oklahoma. They had heard about the beautiful Rio Grande Valley, where they could find work, so they moved their families there.

My Uncle Finley, his wife, Thelma, and their children, Bobbie, Barbara, and Sandy; My Uncle Calvin Diggs, his wife, Grace, and their daughter, Helen; my Aunt June and her husband Cecil; My Uncle Ike Yarbrough and his wife Ora; my brother, Seburn, his wife, Lucille, and their daughter, Betty Lou; and my sister Emogene and her husband J. B. Reynolds had all moved there.

Dad, Mom, my sisters, Fannie and Lois, and I had visited them in the valley in 1938 when I was a junior in high school. Since that time, I had seldom seen any of them.

I arrived in Pharr at sundown and asked for directions to Uncle Finley's house at a service station. It was only about 8 blocks away, and it did not take long to walk that far. I found a small house with all the lights on and walked up to the front door. There was no one in the living room. A large cabinet radio was playing. I could see two of my aunts in the kitchen through the connecting door. I could hear talking and laughter. I decided I would go around to the back and surprise them. I walked up onto the back porch, opened the kitchen door, and walked in. I surprised them all right. Such screaming and hollering I have never heard before! They were jumping all over the kitchen. None of the men-folk were there. I began to say I was sorry and started backing toward the door. I think I managed to say "It's me, J.B., Ben, Jake, John! Don't you know me?" When they finally realized who I was and began to settle down, they started asking me how I got in the house. It turned out that all of the men of the family were lying outside in the weeds watching the house, with shotguns pointed at both doors. About that time the men came in with their shotguns. After a few "wows" and "howdys" and some hand-shaking, they explained the situation. My sister, Emogene, and her husband, J.B., had a trailer house that was parked in a little orange grove on Uncle Finley's lot. The night before I had arrived, J.B. heard a noise outside their bathroom window while Emogene was taking a bath. He went outside to find a man standing on a box, peeping in their bathroom window. The man saw J.B. and ran and jumped the back fence and got away. The men-folk were so upset that they were lying in wait for the window-peeper to come back. We will never know if any of them would have shot him if he had come again. But if I had known about that situation, I would never have slipped up to the house like I did. They said they could see me in the shadows but did not know who I was until I opened the screen door and went in.

After a couple of days of sight seeing, Uncle Ike asked me if I would like to help him build a one-car garage. I said "Sure." I welcomed the chance to do something different. Uncle Ike was a carpenter, and a good one. He was contracting small jobs there in Pharr. He even put me on the payroll. We started building the garage the next day. I learned more about carpenter work in the next two weeks than I ever had known. At the end of my two week furlough I began to dread going back to Camp Barkley and doing guard duty. I decided to stay and help Uncle Ike finish the garage.

We finished it the next week. I packed my clothes and said goodbye to my folks. This had been one of my worst 'goof-offs'. It was a big mistake. I was AWOL. I might be put in the stockade and be guarded instead of guarding the prisoners. I made another big decision before I reached San Antonio. I would return through Houston, Beaumont, and go into Louisiana and find my company and report to my company commander and tell him the truth. The truth is always the best way. When I reported, my captain said I was supposed to be in Camp Barkley. He did not have my records and he could not keep me in the company. What a mess I was in. I went into the bivouac area and visited some of my friends. I did not tell them about the trouble I was in.

Before long, the Captain sent for me. He told me that a trainload of GIs who had been discharged from the field hospital nearby was being sent back to Camp Barkley. He advised me to go down to the train station the next morning and board that train. He also told me not to let them know who I was or that I was on the train and above all else not to mention his name. I boarded the train with the other GI's without being noticed. There were six coaches full.

We were two days and one night getting to Camp Barkley. The

meals were prepared box lunches. Three quartermaster sergeants were aboard to deliver them. Each meal time they came up one meal short. When they finished delivering lunches they came back through, counting soldiers. When I saw them coming, I went into the toilet and stayed until they had passed our coach. On the second day after they delivered lunches, they came through with the list of names of the soldiers who were supposed to be on the train. I went to the toilet again be fore they entered our coach. They did not think to look where I was hiding.

When we reached Camp Barkley I reported to the captain of the guard at the brig. I told him the truth, how I hated to come back to guard duty. How I went to Louisiana to my own company, and how my commanding officer said there was nothing he could do because he did not have my file and because I was not under his command. The captain never asked how I returned to Camp Barkley, nor did I volunteer that information. He said he would take no action against me. The 45th would be back to camp in a week. He would transfer my papers and me to my own company and my company commander could take care of the AWOL charge. Until then, I was assigned to corporal of the guard of my squad. I was returned to my company when they returned. Nothing was ever mentioned to me about the charges against me. I had dodged the bullet. I was so relieved and so grateful that it made a better soldier of me, and made me try harder to do my duties as a soldier. I do not recommend that kind to conduct for anyone. If I had been court-martialed for being AWOL it would have turned my good life completely around. How often the little things in life can become so important. As my dad always said, "Look before you leap".

In March of 1942, the 45th division was moved to Fort Devens, Massachusetts, by train. Riding on a train was boring, especially when there was no place to sleep except sitting in a passenger seat. There was nothing else to do except play poker with the gamblers. I certainly did not do that. I was too conservative to gamble, and I had allotted almost all of my paycheck to my dad for safekeeping. I was always glad when we reached our destination. There was always the rocking motion, the continuous clack of the rails, and the constant passing of scenery by the window. I remember going through Amarillo and Chicago and lots of beautiful farming land along the way. After two days and nights, we arrived at the train station just outside of Fort Devens.

CHAPTER 8
Fort Devens - Yankee Country

This was the first time that the 45th division had barracks to live in. We began close order drill immediately. I suppose that was to get the kinks out after that long train ride. Then we eased into reviews of radio and telephone communication procedures. We also had a couple of full dress reviews on the parade grounds with generals from around the New York and Washington D.C. areas. Soon we started commando courses. The army engineers had built four huge walls between camp and a hog-back ridge close to our camp's border. They were about 50 feet high and 50 feet long. There was a rope ladder made of one-inch rope that covered each wall, from one end to the other and from the ground, over the top, to the ground on the other side. These walls simulated the side of a ship with a one-inch rope net extending  down the side. It was a regular daily exercise for the whole battalion to go scale the four walls with full field pack. A group of ten or twelve men would be started at a time, then another dozen would follow. Sometimes there would be thirty soldiers going up one side of the wall and thirty going down the other. It was real tricky because the rope ladder would give this way and that with every step that was taken.

In the evenings, we went to a large public swimming pool. Everyone had to be able to swim. Each one had to swing out over the pool on a rope and drop into the water and swim out. If anyone could not swim, they had to go back and take lessons until they learned how. This was no problem for me. I learned to swim at an early age. My brothers and I had gone swimming in the river and in farm ponds many times and my brother threw me in deep water and told me to swim. I always appreciated my brothers teaching me so much that I would need in life, and this was no exception. I learned how to swim very quickly. I had also taken swimming at the University of Central Oklahoma for a credit the year I went to college.

My three friends and I started going to Boston on weekend

passes when the Boston Red Sox were playing at home. One of the Saturday games we went to really stuck out in my memories. The Red Sox were playing the New York Yankees in Boston and the great Ted Williams was playing left field for Boston while the "Yankee clipper", the great Joe Dimaggio, played center field for the Yankees.

On one occasion, after a baseball game in Boston, we went to a nice restaurant and had a steak dinner, our favorite pastime. Then we went to the bus station to go back to camp. The last bus left at 1 o'clock a.m.. We arrived at the station early around 11:30pm. It was my turn to pay the taxi driver so my friends went ahead to get their tickets. After I paid for the taxi I went inside and got in line to buy my bus ticket. The bus was already waiting outside with the motor running. My three buddies were in line ahead of me and when they bought their tickets, they went out and got on the bus. As I stepped up to buy my ticket, a guy bumped me from behind. I turned around to find five artillery soldiers behind me. The smell of alcohol was real strong on their breath. The guy who bumped me told me to "watch it" and called me a curse word. I did not feel that I had done anything wrong or that I should be called bad names so I shoved him up against the counter and told him that was not very nice. Suddenly all five guys surrounded me and one of them said, "If you don't like it, just step outside and we will see about that."

I was not about to back down even though I had never faced these odds before. They kept me surrounded as we walked out the back door. I glanced toward the bus as we left and my buddies were already on the bus. There was a bright street light across the alley. We walked to the light and squared off. By that time, all of them were cursing me. Before anyone threw a punch, I heard a voice say; "Long John! What's going on?" I turned to see the platoon sergeant and four of the young soldiers from "B" company that were in my squad back at Camp Barkley when I was assigned to train them there. I told my Indian friends "These guys want to fight me." The sergeant said, "Five on one is too many. Do you think you could get them on us, Long John?" As he spoke, all five of my friends from B Company drew their hand out of their pockets with switchblades opened. The five artillery boys broke and ran down the alley into the dark. They did not seem to be quite as drunk as they had acted before. They also missed their bus. My five friends from B Company laughed so hard they almost got down in the street. I was mighty happy to see them and just at the right time. They had come in the bus station just as we went out the back door and had quickly decided something was wrong, and had decided to see if I was in trouble. It is always good to have friends like them. We went inside and bought our tickets in time to board the last bus back to camp. I had a good visit with them on the way to camp. I had not seen them since we left camp Barkley. Three of the young men that had been in my squad had been promoted to corporal. I thought they deserved the promotion and I was mighty proud of them. They were good soldiers. They told my buddies about the incident in the alley and every little while they would break out in a chuckle about the artillery guys dashing down the alley.

We soon received a lot of recruits right out of boot camp. There were enough to fill the division to full war time strength. All of the new guys were from surrounding states; mostly New York, New Jersey and Pennsylvania. Although they had a different outlook on life from ours they were some good guys. They pronounced words differently, made fun of the way we talked, and made fun of the names of some of the towns in Oklahoma such as Okmulgee. They

Cpl. Frank Latche

also thought we were still fighting Indians and robbing stagecoaches back in Oklahoma and Texas. They were surprised when I told them there was a company of Indians in our regiment. All in all we got along pretty well. Some of the new guys who made good soldiers were Frank Latche, Bob DeAngelo, Whitey Ewanizik, George Hart, Gish Geshwandtner, Eastam Kuchamba, Miller Lackey, George Davis, 'Linkey' Hartz Dunlap, and the list goes on and on. These were some of

the new men who were assigned to my platoon, and they served with me after I was promoted to platoon sergeant. Every one of them was a fine soldier. These were in addition to the guys who came with me from Texas.

Not much later, there was a big change in the communication department. They formed platoons

The Author & Eastam Kuchamba

and transferred one to each battalion. I was promoted to staff sergeant and was transferred to 2nd Battalion and was platoon sergeant of that communication section. It was a good promotion for me and I was eager to meet the challenge. The big problem was that I was no longer under the command of the best officers in the whole dad-gummed army. Captain Murray was promoted to major, and Lieutenant Watkins took his place as company commander with a promotion to captain.

Chapter 9
Training for Amphibious Landing

With my promotion and the changes in the communications department, I would be separated from my three best friends forever. That was the worst part. On the flip side, there were some good men in my platoon at 2nd Battalion headquarters. Lieutenant Neckada was my platoon leader. He was a very good officer. He and I got along swell. He let me handle the personnel in the platoon, and he dealt with the upper echelons. He was from upper New York State.

2nd Battalion was moved to Cape Cod, near Hyannas Port, in May. We camped out on the beach. We would be given two weeks training in shore-to-shore maneuvers using landing personnel boats. Each boat could carry one platoon of 48 men. There were enough boats to carry the whole battalion. The boat would run up on the beach and they'd let the ramp down. We walked on board, the boatswain raised the ramp, and the boat backed off the beach and took us out to sea where they circled the boats in prearranged waves and waited for the signal to go ashore. In our case, each company was a wave. When the signal came to go ashore, the first wave headed for the beach at high speed. In a few minutes the second wave got the message to follow the first wave, and so on until all five waves were on their way. The boats in each wave were about 50 yards apart and each wave had a certain beach to land on. When we beached and the ramp came down, we filed out in an orderly fashion so that no one would be trampled. It was a simple operation that could really be fouled up, unless there was complete understanding and cooperation among the battalion commander, each boatswain, and the company commander. That is why we had to practice so many times. We were to hit the beach running with weapons and full field pack as if we were attacking the enemy from one island to another. It was new to us and it was fun. Sometimes we made 3 or 4 trips to sea each day. We soon began to take this seriously. Word was going around that we soon would be going to the South Pacific to fight island-to-island warfare.

The army personnel hoped there would be no foul-ups if we ever had to do this amphibious exercise in battle against a real enemy, and so did I. Each time we landed, we ran a few yards across the beach and dove to the prone position. After all the boats had beached, we were assembled and the observers went over the mistakes that were made or the correct things they observed. Then we got up, reorganized, and went out again. We were scheduled to be in training there for two weeks, but when our two weeks were finished someone decided that we had done such a good job that the battalion should stay all summer and be observers for the rest of the division. Eight more battalions at two weeks each and that would be all summer long, until September. What a time we had teaching the other men what we had learned, what to do and what not to do.

Just before the evening meal each day our company went swimming at a private beach nearby. Safety precautions were the order of the day, no horseplay, no fooling around. It was very important to concentrate on what we were doing. The troops were supposed to imagine that the enemy was firing at them when we reached the beach.

The first day three guys from my platoon and I went swimming in the evening. We swam out to the buoys that marked the ship channel. We hung on to the buoys and watched a large ship go by toward New York Harbor to our west. We were over half a mile from the beach. We were so far out that the guys back on the beach looked like ants running around.

After a while we swam back to the beach. A lieutenant was waiting for us when each of us walked up onto the beach saying, "The old man wants to see you in his tent now". It was only then that I remembered the commanding officer had told us to not go farther out than 100 yards. The officers escorted us all to the C.P. tent. It was a long hard walk. All the way I was thinking, "Why did I do this? Why did I not remember what the orders were? What is going to happen to us? Will we be busted?" After al,I I was a staff sergeant and was supposed to be a leader. It was too late to worry about it. I was pretty sure we were all going to be busted when the colonel started chewing us out. We were standing at attention in our underwear. The colonel talked slowly and deliberately for about twenty minutes. I never knew before that day how many ways discipline, following orders, and responsibility could be described. After a long while he hesitated, and I thought, "Here it comes." He said, "For what you four have done today, I order you to be life guards for the company every day for the duration of our stay here. You are not to go in the water except to help someone in an emergency situation. Dismissed!" We spent the rest of the summer being lifeguards and thinking about what we should not have done.

One Sunday evening, I went over to the public beach nearby.

I met a young lady from Boston named Claire. She was a bright young lady and we had a pleasant talk. I had never been that impressed with a girl before. It was the last day of her vacation. I asked her if I could come to see her in Boston after we returned to Ft. Devens. She said that would be fine, and gave me her address. She was fascinated with the stories I told her about growing up on a farm in Oklahoma. She also thought we were still fighting Indians in the western states.

That fall, after we returned to camp, I took a weekend pass and went to Boston to see Claire. Their home was a two-story apartment, nothing fancy, just clean and comfortable. There was a one-car garage on the ground floor. Claire was an only child, and lived at home with her mother and dad. She worked in an office downtown as a secretary. I could tell, even when I met her at the beach, that she was a very sheltered child with fine morals. That was the main reason I was attracted to her. Her mom met me at the door, invited me in, and led me to the family room in the back, where Claire and her dad were waiting. Her father was a small, quiet man. He had a 9:00 to 5:00 job at a bank downtown. He never said much and I soon knew why. Claire's mother talked all the time and dominated the conversation. Her mother was dressed like she was going to a party. She had on a real nice evening gown, with jewelry around her neck, on all her fingers, and both wrists. She also had on make-up. She took over the conversation, asking me all kinds of questions. She asked about my army career and my future possibilities with the army, my education and whether I would continue my education some day. She asked about my religion, my family, life on the farm, and on and on. I had nothing to hide. I am who I am, take it or leave it. I never have been one to make changes over night. I answered her questions as best I could. The ones about the future I could not answer because we never know what the future may bring. I would have rather discussed these things with Claire. But I did not get my "rathers". Claire seemed to be embarrassed for her mother's interrogation. I decided she was just an over-protective mother, and let it go at that.

After a long while, Claire's mother told her to come and help her prepare dinner. Dinner to this old farm boy was the noon meal; the evening meal was called "supper" back home. But I understood the difference in culture, and made no comment on that. Dinner was a quiet and elaborate affair. All the dishes and silverware were expensive, to say the least. There were two knives, three forks, and two spoons. There were fine, engraved plates and fancy crystal. The food was delicious. I remember that we had chicken fricassee. It was my first time to have that. The only way I knew chicken was ever cooked was fried or baked. Everything went well, as far as I could tell. I glanced at Claire often and followed her lead on what silverware to use on each dish. I think we had 5 courses. Claire's mother smoked one cigarette after another, in a long cigarette holder. As soon as we were through eating, she put another cigarette in her mouth and hesitated. I took the hint and picked up the lighter and lit her cigarette. She seemed real pleased with that.

When they put the dishes away, the four of us got in the family auto and went to the movies. When we came out of the theater, Claire's mom said Claire and I could walk home. It was the first time she and I had been alone all day. Her mother reminded us not to be long. It was just a few blocks to her home. When we arrived they were waiting for us on the front porch. It was just as well, because it was getting close to the time the last bus would leave for camp. So I just said goodbye and left. For the next few days, I had mixed emotions about Claire's mother.

I never saw Claire again. I remembered the beautiful "dinner" table, white linen tablecloth and napkins, and more silverware and crystal than I had ever seen on a table before. Even though I enjoyed the food, I was not at ease in that atmosphere.

Chapter 10
Pine Camp, New York

I did not have much time to dwell on my weekend or Claire. The following week we were ordered to move to Pine Camp, New York, by truck convoy. Pine Camp was in upper New York State, on the St. Lawrence River near Watertown, as far north as you can go in New York. Again we had barracks to live in and my platoon was housed on the second floor. The very next Saturday night after we arrived, some of us went to the camp theater and saw a movie. When we came out it was snowing huge snowflakes, so thick you could not see very far. The ground was already covered and we did not see the ground again while we were there. We left in March and the snow was still deep. On the way back to the barracks, I cut across the parade grounds. As I came to B Company barracks there was a large

Pvt. Huey Long Shoveling the snow at Pine Camp, NY

crowd out by the boiler. I came closer and I could see they were in a big circle and there was a fight going on in the middle of it. I edged my way in to where I could see. Two young Indians were "duking it out". One was beat up pretty badly. When the other guy would knock him down, everyone would say "Get up! Get up!" in mean voices. Someone would then help him up and shove him back to the center of the ring. After I saw that this soldier was unable to defend himself, I asked the guy next to me if they should not stop the fight. All the guys were wearing parkas with the hood pulled over their heads so I had no idea that I was talking to one of my friends that was in the squad I was in back at B Company at Camp Barkley. He turned to me and said, "Long John, this is a private affair. This soldier was caught stealing from the one who is whipping him. This is our way of punishing him. The fight will not be stopped as long as he can be helped up and shoved back in the ring." I said goodbye to my friend and went on my merry way having learned something new about Indian culture.

Snowplows cleaned the streets and roadways, but the snow kept coming down day and night. One night a fierce blizzard blew in. We could hear the wind howling, and the next morning the snowdrifts were up to our second story windows and the temperature was 35 below zero. We found shovels in the boiler room and dug tunnels through the snow to the mess hall. After the snow was packed on the streets, we checked out ice skates from the quartermaster and skated every where we went. That is where I learned to ice skate. We had classes in the barracks each day, went on hikes down the road twice a week, and went to a movie at the base theater every night. I never went into Watertown, except to get on the train the next March when they moved us to Camp Picket, Virginia, and when I went home on furlough in December. I rode the train all the way to Oklahoma City. The train from Chicago to Oklahoma City was a non-stop flyer that averaged 100 miles an hour. That was a ride I have not forgotten. Some of the married men's wives came to live in Watertown. Their husbands could get overnight and weekend passes to be with them.

Rumors soon began to fly about why we were in camp. Some said we were learning to live in that cold weather so that we would be prepared to go to Iceland, Greenland, or Norway and fight our way south through northern Germany. Some said we were going to Alaska and on through the chain of islands and attack Japan from the north. All turned out to be just rumors. We spent Christmas there and we got Christmas Day off. It was the loneliest Christmas I can ever remember. I put on my ice skates and went to see my

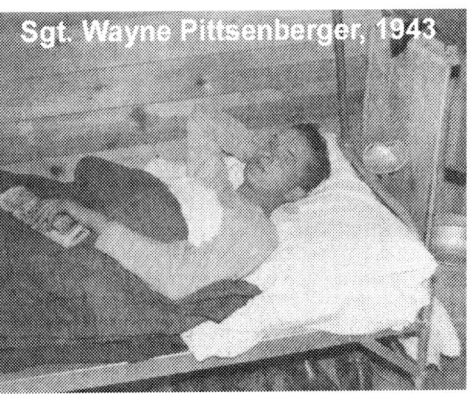
Sgt. Wayne Pittsenberger, 1943

old buddies at Regimental Headquarters Company and 3rd battalion headquarters. Pittsenberger was in the barrack building in bed with the flu. He did not want to go to the hospital. Bill Wier and John Juby were okay. We had a few good laughs. I did not know it at that time, but that would be the last time I would ever see them.

In March, there was still plenty of snow on the ground. We left Pine Camp by train and moved to Camp Pickett, Virginia. We passed through New York City and it was the highlight of the trip. We were astonished at the sight of the skyscrapers. We passed by New York Harbor and there it was, the Statue of Liberty. That was a beautiful sight. I can understand the thrill the immigrants get when they see that great symbol of liberty and freedom. As we went by I heard someone say "Boys, there she is. She stands for what we are fighting for!" That statement made me take a long look. And many thoughts went through my mind. I had seen so many things and done so much that I would never have seen or done if I had not left the farm. What a wonderful country we have. Not only did we need to protect her, but we had Mom, Dad, brothers, sisters, home and apple pie to think about. There was no doubt in my mind about going wherever they sent us or thought they needed us. I had learned some time before to not put much stock in rumors, but to wait for orders. I was ready to do whatever I could to protect our country, *my* country, from the enemy.

By then I had heard of the Germans overrunning the Balkan states, France, and Denmark. I had also heard of the German concentration camps and the mass slaughter of human beings. People of all ages, whole families, were being forced from their homes to camps, starved to death, slaughtered by firing squads, or used as guinea pigs in medical or surgical experiments. I heard about the "Japs" taking the Philippines and many more islands in the Pacific, about the Bataan March, and about the cruel treatment of our servicemen who became prisoners of war. After the fall of Bataan on April 9, 1942, the Japanese commander, Lt. Gen. Masahura Homma, ordered thousands of the American and Filipino prisoners of war to march some 70 miles from Mariveles, at the tip of Bataan, to the San Fernando concentration camp in the interior of the Philippines. Along this route hundreds of the famished, poorly shod, and fever stricken prisoners perished. The Japanese guards, intoxicated by their victory, committed many horrible atrocities with the consent of their commanders. Along one two-and-a-half mile stretch 62 bodies were discovered strewn on both sides of the road. Prisoners were beaten on their heads with clubs when they attempted to drink from the roadside wells after the Japanese halted them and forced them to sit on the hot pavement. Some of the Japanese soldiers deprived the marchers of their shoes and forced them to march in their bare feet. The prisoners who faltered on the way were bayoneted to death. Once 30 marchers were permitted to fill their canteens in a paddy field and as they did so, the Japanese opened fire on them with machine guns. The prisoners were starved on the way and compelled to lap maggotty water when clear water flowed through spigots. The guards ordered "double time" and then shot those who couldn't keep up with the rest. For all these crimes General Homma was held responsible and in 1946 was tried, convicted, and executed on the testimony of some of his victims who had survived years of prison-camp suffering to see justice done.

These things caused us to want to fight to defend freedom, and a thing called patriotism made us see that this country is worth defending. I wanted to keep those things from happening to the United States of America.

I am sorry to say that there is not as much patriotism around these days as there was back then. When war was declared, everyone wanted to do what they could to help the cause. Young women came out of the homes and went to work in the shipyards, the factories, or wherever they were needed. They learned trades such as welding, riveting, working sheet metal, and mechanics. They helped build ships and airplanes and made weapons and ammunition. Some became nurses and went into the Army Nursing Corps, or went overseas and worked in hospitals or, sometimes, on the front lines. Some women joined the WAVES or the WACS. Some learned to fly and ferried airplanes from one base to another or from the factory to air bases wherever the planes were needed. They took the place of all of the available, healthy, young men who were eligible to join the fighting forces of the service and either volunteered or were drafted into the service. The war could not have been successful without these women.

Now, there are a lot of people in America that do not appreciate what a great country this is. They do not know what it would be like to live in a country like Germany or Japan were before World War II. The citizens of those countries at that time had no rights, and could be hauled off to prison by armed guards for no reason other than religious or political beliefs. A lot of people now think the U.S. Government owes them a living. Some lie and cheat to get on welfare or food stamps instead of getting a job, working hard, and earning a living.

This is the best country in the whole world and it hurts me when people do not appreciate it or when they trample, burn, or disgrace the flag that is a symbol of life, liberty, and the pursuit of happiness in America.

CHAPTER 11
Camp Pickett Virginia - The End Of Training

The rest of the train ride from Pine Camp, New York, was uneventful and we arrived at Camp Pickett, Virginia, to find that we once again would be living in barracks. The change of climate was welcomed by all. We went around in our short sleeves. It was nice and warm, and the countryside was green and beautiful. We wasted no time starting our physical fitness program. There were more mock ship walls with rope nets over them to climb. We went on thirty-five mile hikes with full field pack. We had a little five mile hike we went on every Saturday morning which we called the Rat Race. It was also with full field pack and we completed it in one hour. We hiked up into the beautiful Blue Ridge Mountains with full field equipment, and camped out for two weeks. I suppose they were getting us used to roughing it, sleeping on the ground or in pup tents, eating out of our mess kits, and so on.

When we returned to camp, my good friends Warren Howard, Wayne Pittsenburger and I got a weekend pass and went to town to the train depot in town to ride a passenger train down to Raleigh, North Carolina. We wanted to see what it was like to ride a train that was not crowded with soldiers who had not bathed in several days and to take our meals in the dining car instead of having sack lunches on a troop train. As soon as we reached Raleigh, we caught the next train back. When it stopped in Roanoke, Virginia, we decided that we would go to a movie, then take the bus back to camp that day, instead of staying over until Sunday. When we came out of the theater we had plenty of time to walk to the bus station and catch the next bus.

Sgt. Warren G. Howard

The traffic was heavy, just like it used to be in Lindsay, Oklahoma, on Saturday afternoons. As we walked along Main Street, we heard someone behind us counting cadence, "Hut, two, three, four," and thought it must be one of our friends, or at least someone we knew just trying to get our attention. We stopped and turned around to see who it was and, to my surprise, there were five artillery soldiers. It was one of them who had been doing the counting. We had never seen them before so we said "Hi, fellows," and turned to walk on. As soon as we started walking, the guy started counting again. Now, I believe once can be overlooked; but twice is harassment. It was very annoying. We stopped and turned around again. People who were in hearing distance had already begun to stop to watch. I could see that the artillery boys were slightly inebriated, or drunk. This time, we asked them not to do that any more. I remember one of them replied, "Yeah? See if you can make us stop!", then they used a few curse words on us. Like all the other drunks I had fought, I moved in and tried to get my licks in first, and my buddies followed my lead. The only trouble was that there were five of them and three of us. We had to watch our backsides. By then, a huge crowd had gathered and formed a circle that reached across Main Street and stopped traffic both ways. The artillery boys sobered up quickly. They were not nearly as drunk as they had acted at first. I kept punching this guy and backing him out into Main Street. Finally, I knocked him down and he stayed down, then I went to help my buddies. The artillery boys put up a pretty good fight for a little while, but they soon began to tire. We were in better physical shape than they were and they soon gave up. When they did, the crowd started cheering for us. Even people in cars honked their horns and yelled down the street. We accepted the cheers, took a bow, and went on our merry way.

Claire and I had exchanged letters about every two weeks since we had left Fort Devens. It was nothing special. She discussed her job and her mother and dad and she apologized for her mother quizzing me so much while I was there. I had mixed emotions about Claire. She was a very nice young lady intelligent, bright, with a good sense of humor. We had nice conversations together when her mother was not present, and her dad was quiet and pleasant. But I knew I would not like to be around her mother for very long. I never criticized her or told Claire how I felt about her mother in my letters, but Claire was smart enough to know. I never mentioned that I would like to see her again or anything like that. I only told about the army life we were having and the tough exercises we were going through. I did tell her that we would probably be shipped overseas soon, and that I did not know where we would go. I was careful not to make her any promises. She may have figured that out. The last letter I received from her was in May, 1943, just before we shipped out for overseas. She wrote that one of her mother's friends had a son who was a lieutenant in the Air Force. Her mother had asked him over for dinner, and they had gone to the movies. She hoped I did not mind. Since there was really nothing between us anyway I did not know what to write, so I only wrote that we were going away, and would be gone a long time. I told her I did not know what the future would be and let it go at that.

In a few days we were told that we would make a ship to shore landing in the near future. After my promotion to Staff Sergeant, I made out papers to have all of my paycheck sent home to my Dad except $10.00. That was all I needed. It was enough to buy my toilet articles and shaving necessities. When I made out the form, however, I put down my correct birth year which was 1921. Someone noticed that I had put down November 28, 1920, on my enlistment papers and I was called to the office. I told the Captain exactly what happened; that I had put down that incorrect date so I could enlist when I was only 17 years old. He said that the army was not about to get rid of me for that and I was relieved. He said they would need my birth certificate so they could change the paperwork to show the right birth date, so I wrote to my Dad and asked him to send it to me.

In the last part of April, the division was moved to Norfolk, Virginia with full field equipment. We were loaded onto a troop transport ship that moved up Chesapeake Bay. At midnight, the anchor was dropped. We organized our units on the main deck, went over the side of the ship, climbed down the rope net and into the landing craft. This was the reason we had been practicing climbing the rope nets. From there, the boats took us out away from the ships and attempted to circle the ships in waves. During the maneuvers, a sudden, powerful windstorm struck from the south. The wave formation of the boats became more of a straight line than a circle. The boats circular path was more like a huge paperclip. The boats would struggle along into the wind in a straight line until the lead boat reached the location where we were supposed to circle. It would turn around but the wind was so strong that it blew the lead boat past the line of boats in a hurry. Then it would turn in behind the last boat and struggle back against the wind.

The boats continued to struggle this way for about 3 hours until all personnel had embarked into the LCPs, or Landing Craft Personnel boats. Then our boatswain got the word to head for our assigned beach.

Despite the weather, our wave landed okay on the beach. When the boat beached and the ramp went down, we rushed across the beach and dove to the ground just as we had learned in training. Afterward, we assembled, reorganized, and proceeded to our area. By that time, the wind had changed to the north and it began to snow. Part of our orders was to perform as near to combat conditions as possible, so we dug foxholes. We fell into our foxholes, wrapped up in our blankets and shelter halves, which is half of a pup tent, and tried to get some sleep. We heard at breakfast that some of the boats lost their direction and landed on a beach in Maryland. That was not too bad considering the high winds and that we had no lights.

We had been through shore-to-shore and ship-to-shore landing exercises. We had trained for three years counting one year in the national guards. We learned every phase of infantry training for combat and were taught about every type of modern weapon and troop movement. What next?

We had little time to speculate. As I remember, we were confined to camp. Everyone seemed to know what was happening. There were not even any rumors going around. We spent the next few days requisitioning and replacing equipment lost on the ship-to-shore landing maneuvers. We were told to get our personal business in order, so we did some letter writing. There were a few men who had applied for a discharge because they were over forty years old and some who requested hardship discharges. Those applications were processed at that time. I received my birth certificate from Dad and got my date of birth corrected on my records.

Chapter 12
Life on a Troop Ship

I guess I was a little anxious to use some of the things that we had learned in our training courses. I was also curious about the adventures that were coming but I have to admit I was not prepared for what would happen in war against the enemy. Our training was not at all like the real war.

In a few days trucks moved us to an embarkation camp at Newport News, Virginia. The trucks drove inside the camp to unload us. When we stepped out of the trucks, it was the first and only time I ever felt like I was in prison. There were thirty-foot high barbwire fences all around the camp. When the trucks moved out, the high gate was closed, locked, and guarded by armed guards. We were assigned to a huge tent, large enough for the whole company, with 250 army cots inside. They told us we were bound for North Africa.

The next day we boarded a troop ship and sailed out of the harbor to join the convoy. There were 50 troop ships, 2 destroyers, and a cruiser. It was known that German submarines were cruising the Atlantic Ocean. They had already sunk several ships, and some had been spotted near the coastline of America. Within an hour the convoy started a zigzag course. It was the latest maneuver to avoid torpedoes from enemy submarines. The whole convoy traveled at the same speed in the same direction for one minute. Then all ships would make a 45-degree turn at that time, travel that direction for one minute, and turn back to the original direction for the next minute. It was a sight worth seeing for this old country boy. The zigzagging made the trip twice as long. But if it got us there safely, then it was worth it. It took us 29 days to cross the Atlantic Ocean.

I spent the first night in the hull where the troops slept on the fourth deck in a hammock-type bunk. The bunks were stacked ten high. The rows were so close together only one person could walk between them at a time. By morning, the hull stunk so bad with body odor that I needed some fresh air. I was not looking forward to spending another night down there. Some of the guys were seasick already. Fortunately, the ship's crew was only enough men to operate the ship. They had no security personnel so after chow an officer asked if anyone would volunteer to do guard duty on the ship. I would have done anything to stay out of that stinking hole. I and five others from my platoon raised our hands. The officer called for a meeting and assigned us to our stations, gave us our duties, and made out a schedule. One soldier was to be stationed at each stairway. Two were stationed at each entrance to the galley. The other four would roam the main deck. Our duties were to keep men from crowding the stairways, to take anyone who fell or had an accident to the sick bay, and to caution the men not to run or get reckless on the main deck. Most of all we were to see that everyone went below if, and when, the ship's alert signal was sounded. Just as the meeting was almost over, the officer in charge asked if anyone could climb without becoming dizzy or scared. I had climbed those cottonwood and elm trees back home and it never bothered me, so I raised my hand. I was the only one who did. I was assigned to the crow's nest, a little observation cage 60 feet above the main deck in the middle of the ship. Our assignment was to work four hours and be off eight hours. The view from up there was great. I could see the whole convoy. I watched them zigzag, and watched the semaphore messengers wave their flags from ship to ship to maintain radio silence. We had nice weather all the way. I enjoyed the cool breeze every day. Since I was the only volunteer for the crow's nest, I pretty well set my own hours. Most of the time I stayed up there sixteen hours a day. I even took a few naps. I sometimes stayed until 10 or 11o'clock at night. The five men from my platoon and I found a good place on deck to sleep so we would not have to go back in the hull. We pulled the tarp back on one of the emergency rescue boats on the main deck and crawled in. We even went below and brought our equipment up and stashed it in the boat. I came down from my little cage to sleep and eat, but then climbed back.

During the voyage, the command ship sounded the alarm signal three different times. Everyone had to go below but me. I stayed and watched. The destroyers broke convoy and took off at high speed. As soon as they cleared the last ship they started throwing depth charges from both sides of the ship. Sometimes they went out of sight still throwing depth charges. We never got a report on any of these incidents; but I am certain there was a good reason for doing them.

One night, about 10 o'clock, I was about ready to come down from my post when the general alarm sounded. Every ship in the convoy turned their lights on. There in the middle of the convoy was a huge ship traveling in the opposite direction from the convoy. The strange ship turned its lights on, and there were Red Cross flags all over it. It was a huge hospital ship taking wounded back to the states from Africa. How it got into the convoy without a collision,

I will never know. I do know one thing:if it had hit one of the other ships, it would have been one big mess.

The convoy's direction was southeast and crossed the equator somewhere east of South America. Why we took that route I did not know. There was no one to ask but the deck hands, and they did not know either. It was hot and humid. Soon we turned east for two or three days, then north along the African coast but never close enough to see land.

One day we had high winds and huge waves but no clouds. When the ships turned one way, we had a crosswind. The ship would rock from side to side. When that happened, I could look straight down from the crow's nest into the water. Then the ship rolled to the other side and I could look straight down into the water on that side. The wind continued all day and into the night. I never was seasick.

Early one morning I spotted land almost dead ahead and a little to the right of our main course. Soon, I could see high cliffs with water between them. I knew from my geography that it was the Strait of Gibraltar. The convoy had gotten very close to land when, all of a sudden, the ships danger alarm signal sounded loud and clear. The destroyers took off at high speed to our south side. The convoy made a ninety-degree turn to our left without breaking formation and headed out to sea still zig-zagging.

Those navigators were good. As far as I could tell by the sun and the moon and stars that night, the convoy made a complete circle in 24 hours and came back to the exact location where we were the day before. When I climbed to my crow's nest post the next morning, there was that same view just like a picture, high cliffs on both sides and water in between.

This time we sailed into the Mediterranean Sea and continued east to Algiers. They dropped anchor about a mile off shore. We got our gear together and prepared to make a ship-to-shore landing. This one was in daylight and well behind the front lines .The American and British armies had hemmed up the remains of a defeated German Nazi army in Morocco and were mopping up on them.

The landing went real well. This time we all got to see what everyone was doing. We landed east of Algiers and hiked west through the town to our camp sites about 12 miles from the city. It was deep sand with scattered small trees similar to the mesquite of West Texas.

There was a 5-foot high stone fence from the road running south as far as we could see. The next morning when we arose from our pup tents, we saw hundreds of Algerian men sitting on the stone fence watching us. They were dressed in long, light colored robes with white turbans on their heads, just sitting, watching us. I fired a long burst from my Tommy gun over their heads. They leaped from the fence and dashed madly away, their robes flapping in the breeze behind them. They did not come back again while we were there.

For us it was a time for rest after the long boat ride. It was a time to gather and clean our clothes and equipment and to replace anything that we had lost. It was a time to enjoy a few hot meals. And it was a time to go swimming in the Mediterranean Sea and lie in the sand on the beach for a couple of hours each day while we could.

We made our landing on African soil on June 29th, 1943. On the second day of July we were loaded onto trucks and we traveled to Oran. We boarded a ship there that cruised to the center of Oran harbor and dropped anchor.

Chapter 13
From Oran to Italy

It was still hot and humid and there was no wind. Mountains surrounded the Oran harbor. There was nothing to do but lean on the rail and watch the other troop ships. Some were already loaded and anchored like we were. More ships were being boarded at the docks and even more were coming into the harbor from the sea. We spent the Fourth of July strolling the main deck. It was not a good way to enjoy Independence Day, but that was the routine at Oran harbor until the night of July 8th.

That night, we could hear the engines start and the chain grinding as the anchor was being raised. The ships eased out of the harbor one by one. We could see enough by starlight to tell that they had formed a convoy and were headed east. We did not know where we were going, but we were on our way.

The next morning when we woke, a fierce wind was blowing. Waves were splashing across the main deck. They must have been 20 feet high with big whitecaps. Everyone was below. I went to the top of the stairway and peeked out as one of the deck hands was leaving. Outside, I could see a tugboat traveling with the convoy close to our ship. The waves were so high that the tugboat went completely out of sight each time a wave passed by. It appeared again in the low ebb when the wave passed over. The little tugboat did not bounce or buck, but kept a steady course with our ship and the rest of the convoy. We had a meeting. We were told that we were somewhere north of Egypt, and that our objective was to make a ship-to-shore landing in the early morning hours of July 10th, which was the next day. Our schedule was to anchor off the southwest coast of Sicily and go over the side of the ship at midnight. We were scheduled to land on the beach just before daylight but we were not sure if it would happen or not.

Before the Allied invasion of North Africa, General Mark Wayne Clark was Deputy Commander in Chief of the Allied Forces in the North African Theater. He made a secret and very hazardous trip to Algeria on the submarine SERAPH to gather intelligence for our landing. Soon after his intelligence trip he

Gen. Mark Wayne Clark

became Commanding General of the 5th Army in Italy and it was now his decision as to what we would do next. If the wind continued at that velocity, and the waves were as fierce as they were during our meeting, General Mark Wayne Clark might postpone the landing.

The wind died down in the early hours of the night so we continued to sail west toward Sicily. We arrived at our location at midnight and dropped anchor. The waves were still about 15 feet high, but they were not whitecapping as they were earlier. They were smooth on top. All platoon sergeants were ordered to sick bay. The navy man in charge told us to take our helmet shell off. He then counted out 48 small blue pills about the size of a small bird's egg. He told us to give every man in our platoon one pill. I returned to the main deck and passed out the pills. Some of the men who were "in-the-know" said it was Benzedrine. Some called them "blue dreamers", others called them "I don't give a darn pills". They said they did not effect our mental or physical ability but relieved the anxiety and worry of danger. I guess they thought we needed that on our first landing in enemy territory and I guess we might have. That was the only time they gave us the pills and it was the only time I ever took a pill that was not prescribed by a doctor. While I was passing out the pills, my good buddy and platoon 'philosopher' said (and I will never forget his words) "Long John, the folks back home will never believe that you gave us dope before we went into battle." His name was Colbert Starr from Stillwell, Oklahoma. We had many private talks. His main concern was about who from our platoon would be there and would stand fast when the going got tough. As for me, I had no doubts about any of them. They were all well trained. They took their assignments and did their best, which was always above average.

We lined up by platoons to go over the side of the ship and get in the boats at midnight, as scheduled. We had full field packs and rifles (except for me; I carried a Tommy gun.) Everyone carried four grenades, and everyone had their ammunition belt of bullets. The platoon sergeants were ordered to be the last one of each platoon to go over the side in case someone needed help. There were three rope ladders with three boats being loaded at the same time. Going over the side and stepping into the boat went smoothly for my platoon. When the waves are high like they were that night, stepping off of the net into the boat is all a matter of timing. You watch where the boat reaches its highest point before it suddenly drops to the lowest point. Then you climb down to that point and wait. It only takes a few seconds. You simply step in as the boat pauses at its peak.

I was halfway down the ladder to the loading point when I noticed the sergeant on the rope ladder next to mine was having trouble getting into his boat. I stopped on the ladder and watched. I felt so helpless. There was nothing I could do but watch. He climbed too far down the ladder while the boat was at the bottom of the wave. When the boat came up, the sergeant quickly climbed up too high to keep from being crushed between the ship and the boat. When the boat dropped he climbed down too far again. I watched this happen several times. About the fifth time the sergeant turned loose and leaped into the boat from about four feet above it. The men in the boat caught him and kept him from being hurt. I watched how high the boat rose on the net, stationed myself there until the boat rose again, and stepped in. After we had landed, we heard that two soldiers on other ships were crushed between their ship and the landing craft and were swept away by the sea.

I took my position at the front of the boat beside the ramp. We all knelt down in four rows as we had been trained to do. Our boat went out and joined the other boats of our company that were circling and we waited for orders that it was our time to go ashore.

CHAPTER 14
Sicily - A Taste Of War

I cannot describe the feeling of going toward the beach of a foreign country that was occupied by enemy soldiers. I know how I felt, but I do not know what was on the minds of the forty-eight silent men with me. There were thousands of soldiers in this same situation who made amphibious landings in the South Pacific, and later in Italy and Normandy, France. Thousands died on the beaches. Many of those who survived would never talk about their experiences and I respect them for that. For nearly 50 years I felt the same way. But the depressed feeling does not go away when one does not talk to someone about how he feels. Several years ago, when I began writing notes of the memories of my experiences, I was surprised to find that I could remember it all. When I began to put it all together I decided that my grandchildren might like to read about World War II from someone who was there.

No one said anything on the way to the beach. Sure, I was scared. I remember praying a silent prayer. I asked God to be with me, no matter what happened. I asked Him to give me strength and courage to do the job that I had been trained to do.

Our boat came to a halt like when you stop a car suddenly. I thought it had run up on the beach like it did in practice. But when the ramp came down, we were several feet from the beach. I went down the ramp into the water. It was only about knee deep. I waded toward the beach without a word. I remember glancing back; and everyone was following. There was enough light from the stars to see some small sand dunes and small bushes about 50 yards away. I quickly decided to make a dash across the sand to the bushes and sand dunes. If I were fired on, I would dive to the ground and crawl. That is what we had been taught to do. I took off running as fast as I could.

Halfway to the bushes, I heard this low, coarse voice say, "Long John." I recognized the voice as that of my Indian friend, Colbert Starr. I slid to a stop and answered, "Yeah" in a very low voice. My first thought was that something bad had happened near the water. My second thought was "What if there are machine guns and rifles aimed at me from the sand dunes?" I was a "dead duck". Then I heard the same voice again. This time he said, "Long John, take

Colbert Starr

shorter steps." Now Colbert was very small, only about 5 feet 2 inches tall, and he weighed about 125 pounds. I understood the message loud and clear. He was worried about land mines. He knew that if he could step in my tracks there would be no danger of him stepping on a mine. Well, at least I was good for something. We had a lot of laughs about that later, but it was too serious at that time to be funny to me.

We all made it safely to the dunes, dove to the ground, and looked around and listened. There were no soldiers, no machine guns, no bunkers, and no mines. By then it was daybreak. We searched the dunes and found no tracks except our own, so we assembled on a large flat mound nearby. We could see our ships anchored a half-mile out. The boats were unloading supplies from the ships onto the beach. We were counting the men in each platoon to see if everyone was present and if everyone was all right.

As we were waiting for the battalion commander and his staff to come ashore and give us our orders for the day, two fighter planes suddenly appeared. They were coming fast and low over the edge of the water. They began firing on the beach in front of us where the boats were unloading supplies. As the lead plane drew near, I could see the big black cross on the side. I knew it was a German plane and everyone else must have known, too. The entire battalion reacted at once and started firing. Nine hundred rifles firing at once are hard on the ears. We missed the lead plane; but several rounds hit the second plane as it went by and it started smoking. As we watched the right wing dipped a little and the plane made a slow turn toward the sea. It continued to lose altitude until the wing dipped into the water. Then it took a nosedive into the water and sank immediately near one of our ships. There was no sign of the pilot surviving. Everyone was so happy that they yelled and danced and cheered like a crazy crowd at a ball game.

We were soon told that our objective was a German air base 35 miles inland. A country road nearby led to the air base. Our orders were to capture it and prevent the Germans from using it. We moved out in columns of two toward the country road. We had not turned onto the road when we heard a motor coming from over the small hill. We knew it was not ours so everyone dove to the ground. A small tank, about half as big as our Sherman tanks, came to the top of the hill and stopped. The field where we lay was freshly plowed. We were in plain sight. They could also see the ships anchored off shore and the hundreds of boats unloading supplies onto the beach. What an awesome sight that must have been to the tank crew. It turned around quickly and sped out of sight. The sound died in the distance. We never saw the little tank again. Someone said it was an Italian tank. We dusted off our woolen uniforms and moved out again. We continued down the country road about 15 miles that day and made camp for the night. We did not see any sign of the enemy after the little tank sped away. We were almost halfway to our objective.

It was hot and humid that day, and we were griping about having to wear woolen uniforms. We found out, however, that they felt pretty good after the sun went down. We bedded down and posted guards and I took the first watch. Very few of the men used their shelter half to make a tent. Most of them spread it on the ground to lie on it. We had strict orders to have a complete black-out. That meant no lights of any kind, not even lighted matches or cigarettes. Once again, the sky was clear and the stars gave enough light to keep from running into anything. The officers' orderlies made their tents for them and there was a black-out tent for the command post where the officer of the guard stayed. That night there was a very bad foul-up in communications. I have never seen any thing written about it in the history of the Sicilian campaign or in the *Stars and Stripes*. I am quite sure someone prevented it from being published, and it is just as well. Soon after dark, all the sergeants of the guard that were on duty at that time were called to the black-out tent. The officer in charge said that he had received a message from army headquarters that was sent through Regimental headquarters. He read it to all of us aloud. The message was, "Beware of paratroopers."

I went back and told every guard on my shift that there might be a paratroop attack during the night. Within an hour we heard the drone of many airplane engines. They were coming from the southwest, from the sea and from the direction of Africa. I thought that was a little odd, but in war odd things happen. The roar of the planes got louder as they came near. Soon we could see the dim outline of the planes by the light of the stars. They were a little east of my company's location. As they came about even with us, I could make out the image of many white parachutes behind each plane.

They were out of our range, but within the range of the company just east of us. That company started firing and continued the rifle fire until one of the paratroopers landed and identified himself as an American. Somehow they got the barrage stopped and none too soon. We were told the next morning that 13 American troopers were wounded. None were reported dead. Miracles do happen, even in war.

We were awakened at daylight the next morning and were on our way to our objective shortly thereafter. It doesn't take long to eat a K-ration. About mid-morning my company was passing a small house by the side of the road. It was made of stone with a red tile roof. That type of house was very common in that country. There was no door in the side of the building next to the road but there was a window in the center of the wall. Suddenly machine gun fire broke the silence. Bullets whizzed overhead. Everyone dove for a shallow ditch that the rain had washed out on the opposite side of the road. I rose up enough to see the house. I could see smoke coming out of the window. One of the officers of our company called out "Sergeant Worley, can you tell where the gun shots are coming from?" I told him it was coming from the house as I jumped up and ran back across the road to a tree that was in the front yard. No one fired at me so I raced to the corner of the house. I pulled a concussion grenade from my pouch and pulled the pin. I started counting to five by ten thousands just like we had been taught. I ran toward the window. I had counted to three-ten thousand by the time I got there. I threw the grenade in the window and kept running. By the time I reached the other corner the grenade went off. Pieces of tile went ten feet above the roof. A cloud of red dust rose out of the house. Pieces of tile landed all over the yard. There was very little of the roof left on the house. There was no window on the north side of the house so I ran to the next corner and peeked around to see what I could see in the back. I saw a corporal and a private from G Company looking at me from the next corner. As we waved at each other, a soldier in Italian uniform staggered out the back door. We all three drew our sights down on him, but no one fired. He took a few steps and fell headfirst. His

A typical farmhouse at Anzio

head and shoulders and arms were covered with blood. He tried to raise his head. He moaned and fell back down took a deep breath and did not move again

The soldiers from G Company met me at the only door to the house. Dust was still thick inside. We entered anyway one at a time, commando style. A table, some stools, pots, pans, and broken tile were scattered everywhere. The door between the two rooms had been blown off and was lying next to the back door. We peeped through the doorway. Broken tile was everywhere. Two bodies and a machine gun covered with blood and tile lay on the floor by the window. The men wore Italian uniforms. They did not move. They were dead.

I went outside and around the house to the road and called out, "All clear!" Our men began to get up and get back on the road. They were cheering and waving as far down the road as I could see, but I did not feel like cheering. I was thinking of the expressions on the faces of the three dead Italians. I had never seen a dead man before. I did not dare show my true feelings. I was thinking that, after all, I was supposed to be these soldiers' fearless leader. Army training can mold people into characters that they have never been before or that they had never thought they could be. I had talked many times with the men in my platoon about things like this-about courage, about being brave in dangerous situations, about who would be there for each other when the going got rough. I was not about to show any weakness now that the incident was over. I had read somewhere that "War is hell," and most of it is. But somebody has to do it. It was comforting to know we had no casualties from the machine gun attack.

As we continued our march down the road toward our objective, the captain doubled our point guard and dispatched a squad on each side of the road to keep abreast of us and to guard our flank. During the march I had time to think about why we were there and it helped me calm down after the excitement. The extra guards had time to investigate buildings and other places where someone might be hiding.

That afternoon, while we were taking a ten minute break, the major came up the road in his jeep. His driver stopped beside us and the major was telling our commanding officer that we were getting close to the airport so we would change our approach. Instead of marching in the road in columns of two, we were to spread out in combat formation, be real quiet, and stay hidden in the grass and weeds, even if we had to crawl. We were to keep in close contact with G Company, who would be to our right, and advance under cover. The terrain was almost level, slightly rolling, and covered with waist-high grass and weeds with trees and bushes everywhere.

We were talking with the major's driver nearby when, very suddenly, we heard the sound of large engines in the distance ahead. The major slid over under the steering wheel and took off, floorboarding the jeep into a sharp right turn, and throwing dust and dirt all over us. He headed down the road to the rear, leaving his driver behind with us. The sound of the motors was getting louder. We knew it had to be enemy tanks because General Patton and all of our American Sherman tanks had landed many miles to our left.

I looked at Warren Howard, and he looked at me. We both had the same idea. There was a huge tree right beside the road with large thick leaves. We both started running for the tree at the same time. A large limb had grown out over the road. We climbed the tree and climbed out over the middle of the road on the big limb. I looked to see where the rest of the platoon was. They were behind a stone fence that ran from the right side of the road. It was about 3 feet tall and every man was crouched behind the fence about 5 feet apart from each other, leaning against the fence, with their rifles resting on the fence in the ready-to-fire position. Two German Tiger tanks came over the little hill about two hundred yards from us. They stopped beside each other and idled their engines as they swung their turrets back and forth, observing. They stayed there for about two minutes, but it seemed like an eternity. Finally, they turned and sped away, out of sight. We never saw them again. We moved out into the pasture until we contacted G Company. We spread out to about 10 feet apart and started moving forward through the grass and weeds. As we got to the top of the small hill where the two tanks had stopped and turned back, we could see the top of a stone building with a red tile roof. There was another stone fence running eastward from the road as far as we could see. We could also see several large sheds with no sides to the east of the house. On top of the house was a flagpole with a black flag flying at the top. There was not much wind but occasionally the wind would blow and the flag would rise. When it did we could see a cross in the middle. There was no guard tower, and we could not see anyone because of the stone fence. We began to crawl through the grass very quietly.

When we reached the stone fence and peeked over it we saw several men unloading boxes from a large flatbed truck onto a platform near the back door of the house. We were only about 50 yards from them. Other men were working on two airplanes under some sheds nearby. About a dozen fighterplanes were staked down near the runway. They were all Luftwaffe with black crosses on the fuselage. We had not been discovered. There were no guards on the lookout tower. The Germans did not suspect a thing.

An officer down the fence from us yelled "Fire!" Every man pushed his weapon across the stone fence and opened fire. Once again, the sound of our nine hundred guns was deafening. The Germans panicked. Some froze in their tracks in disbelief. Some started running in different directions. Several in dress uniforms ran out the back door. They were probably officers or pilots. The truck driver floorboarded the truck. It was headed straight toward my platoon. There were 3 or 4 men standing up on the truck bed holding on to the cab. The driver tried to turn toward the main gate. But he was killed instantly. The men on the truck bed were shot several times and fell off the truck. The truck went out of control and turned over on its side. Shooting continued until there was no one standing or even moving. It was all over in a matter of minutes but the hardest part was yet to come. We received orders to "Go make sure they are all dead". I wondered to myself, "What will happen if they are not all dead?", but I jumped over the stone fence without saying anything. When I landed on the other side, I found that my whole platoon had jumped over with me.

I went to the front door of a house that had been serving as a German office. Colbert Starr and Warren Howard were with me. We entered commando style, one at a time. We went into each room the same way but found no one in the house. Many dead Germans lay at the back door. Twelve German fighter planes would never shoot an Americans again. We camped close by in the pasture that night. One half of the platoon stood guard until midnight and the other half relieved them and guarded the campsite until daylight. We did not know how many enemy soldiers were in the area or their location.

I took the second shift of guard duty, midnight until daylight. We all dug foxholes. I got in mine and tried to sleep, but I was too keyed up. I decided that I would give thanks to God for letting me live through these first two days of combat. I remember that prayer until this day. I asked Him to not let me die or be buried in a foreign country. My folks would not know how I died, if I suffered, or where I was buried, and I did not want that.

I did not ask Him to protect me from harm, hunger, exhaustion, or wounds. I just did not want a messenger going to my home, telling my folks, "I am sorry, but your boy is dead." For some reason, I thought of that when I looked at those 17 young German airmen that evening. Seventeen mothers would be waiting somewhere in Germany for a letter from their sons. That letter was never going to come. I did not want that to happen to my folks. That was only part of the prayer. I prayed to God that if He would see that I returned home alive, I would witness in His name all of my life. He made good my request. Sometimes I feel that I have slacked off with doing my part. I am glad that He is a forgiving God.

Every one was awakened at daylight the next morning. This had been discussed many times in our training and pep talks. The enemy was most likely to attack at daylight than any other time of the day or night hoping to catch us asleep or unaware. We assembled in columns of two and moved out at sun up. As we passed by the main gate to the airport we could see the bodies of the dead Germans lying where they fell. It was not a pretty sight. All that I could think was "This is war." What happened on those two days was what we had been trained for. Our mission was to prevent these enemies from attacking the United States of America and keep them from taking over our land and our homes and even enslaving our families like they already had done on this little island of Sicily and in several countries in Europe.

As we marched northward, down that two track dirt road, there was no doubt in my mind that I would certainly go home alive to my family but I had no idea when that would be or what would happen to me before I got there. I remember believing that God would take care of me. I did not worry about the things that could happen to me, but neither did I throw caution to the wind. I was just as scared as the other men were. I remembered my dad saying many times that everyone had a guardian angel; and I believe that with all my heart. I do not believe that I would be here alive today if it were not so. Sure, I was scared when artillery and mortar shells exploded nearby and shook the ground around me or when bullets or shrapnel whizzed by my head but I tried not to show fear before the men. I have always believed that fear is contagious. All of my men felt the same way. As their platoon sergeant, I always made an extra effort to be calm and cool in every dangerous situation. I tried to consider what was best for the entire platoon. They all seemed to trust my judgment. I never asked anyone to do anything that I would not do. I liked to take the lead, to be out in front. I wanted to know what was happening and help decide what to do. I think that my being single was in my favor. I think that if I had had a wife and children at home at that time, I would have been more cautious. Everyone in my platoon did his share. They were there when they were needed and they did what they were trained to do. I had the honor and privilege to serve with the bravest men in the army.

Just a few days later Mussolini was executed. Italy and Sicily were no longer allies of Germany. In fact, two or three Italian regiments joined us in Italy a few months later to help us fight the Germans. I tried to remember that countries had been fighting and killing each other since

Benito Mussolini & Adolph Hitler

the beginning of time and thinking that way helped me to cope somehow with the happenings of this terrible war.

As we moved north along the country road at a steady pace, we stopped only now and then for a ten minute break. The four rifle companies were ahead of us. The lead company had a point guard spread out in front to try to prevent an ambush. Each company had flank guards on both sides of the road to detect any sign of a counter-attack. I took the left flank position of our company. I walked through the pastures and fields about 100 yards from the column which was close enough to see the troops. We heard shots ahead at the head of the column and the troops stopped for a few minutes, then continued walking. About a mile from there, I walked out of a pasture into a field of maize about waist high. I could see a rifle butt with a GI helmet hanging on it showing above the maize. I walked down the turn row to where I could see down the row that the helmet was on. I saw a body lying between the two rows and when I reached the site I recognized the soldier. He was one of a pair of twin brothers in H Company. He had been shot between the eyes. The helmet on top of the rifle with the bayonet stuck in the ground was to mark the location for the burying crew who would come later and do their job. This young man was the first casualty of our regiment. Until the day before this I had only seen two dead people in my lifetime. One was my Grandma Evans and the other was my cousin Don Worley's stillborn baby. There was nothing I could do so I waved to the company and continued on my way.

The climate there that summer was similar to the summer climate in East Texas: hot and muggy. When we took the next break, I strolled over to the road where the men were resting. The main line of talk was that everyone had emptied his canteen and there was no extra water. G Company was just ahead of us. Some of them were lying in the shade of a tree with some of our guys. One soldier from G Company was lying with his feet crossed. He laid his rifle along his leg pointed at his instep and said, "Boys, I'm going home," and pulled the trigger. The break was over. We got back on the road and moved out. The platoon leader from the boy's company called the company medic to give him first aid and we left them there.

We knew there were some enemy troops up ahead so we moved very quietly and cautiously. About noon, we came to a house by the side of the road. The point guard searched the house. It was empty. There was an old fashioned dug well with an oak bucket in the front yard. I walked over to the well. A couple a dozen men had gathered around it. They had drawn a bucket of water and were filling canteen cups, some drinking, some filling their canteens. If it had not been so crowded I would have been right up there in the crowd. A lieutenant from one of the rifle companies shouted for everyone to move away from the well. "NOW!" When everyone had moved to the road, four men who were trained for special duty came and started probing for mines. They found six personnel mines evenly spaced about 10 feet from the well made in a circle. They called them "Bouncing Betties." They were all buried and covered with dirt. They had prongs that served as triggers. If someone stepped on a prong, a small explosion occurred, shooting the mine up about waist high. The main charge exploded, sending hundreds of small rounds in all directions. It is said that they could almost cut a person in two. We all learned a valuable lesson that day in personal safety, one that we should have already known. We were lucky that no one set off a mine. We were also supposed to purify native water with purifying tablets before drinking it. Everyone had tablets, but no one remembered to use them.

As we walked in pursuit of the enemy, I thought of Sergeant Gregory's predictions when we were in our winter camp near

McAlester, Oklahoma, in 1939. One part of his theory had come true, *"the United States always goes to war after having a winter camp."* The other part of his prediction was that *"being in a communication platoon was a safe place to be."* He went on to say that we would be far behind the front lines, and that there was nothing to worry about. I could not go along with that one.

We marched all day in that same formation, columns of two, with point guard and flank guards out. We took ten minute breaks each hour, then we would get back to pursuing the enemy. That night, at about 10 o'clock, the point guard came upon a roadblock. Several shots were exchanged. We all dove to the ground by the side of the road. It was dark, except for the starlight. It was scary not being able to see or to know how many enemy troops were up ahead or where they would attack. The two things that concerned me the most were hand-to-hand combat and poison gas. I still remembered those four World War I veterans telling about those two things happening to their company in France.

We lay there just listening to the gunshots and some men shouting. Soon we heard a big motor start up, like a big truck motor. It sped away in a hurry and went out of hearing distance. Word was passed back to us that there were no casualties and that everything was fine. We continued our pursuit of the enemy until after midnight. For the next several days we moved north. Our troops were to our right and to our left and were staying alongside of us. Every day the point guard ran into a roadblock. A few shots were fired and then the enemy would move out. We knew that was a delaying maneuver. But we did not know why. We learned after the campaign was over that the Germans were moving all troops, tanks, and artillery to the northeastern point of Sicily. They moved them across the narrow channel to the tip of the toe of the Italian mainland, or the "boot" as it was called, and they were trying to slow us down all that they could.

One day we reached a rock fence overlooking a pretty little valley. We stopped in the shade of some trees for a break. The valley was only a quarter of a mile wide with only short grass for ground cover. Our battalion commander decided that it could be a trap. He sent G company to our left to go down another way and cross the valley then come back to counter attack if the enemy was waiting for us on the other side. In a little while, Lieutenant Baldwin decided that G Company should have had enough time to cross the valley and get back even with us but we had no communication with them. So he told his driver to bring the jeep to him. He and his driver, Huey, drove down the road to cross the valley. There was a shallow dry ditch halfway across. As they started to cross the ditch, we heard a mortar fire. We heard the screaming missile as it rose high in the air. We could tell by its sound that it was not going to reach us; so we continued to watch Lieutenant Baldwin and Huey. Lucky for them they heard it too. Huey stopped the jeep and they both jumped out and dove into the ditch. The mortar shell landed in the middle of the big white star on the hood and blew the jeep to pieces. When the shrapnel, Jeep parts, dust, and smoke cleared Huey and Lieutenant Baldwin got up and walked away without a scratch. A big German truck started up and sped over the hill and out of sight.

As we continued our march across Sicily, the road we were following turned to the northeast up a winding mountain road.

We shortly came to a small village high up in the mountains. We were advancing in combat formation and were fired on as we reached the first building. G Company was to our left. They circled to the other end of the street. Three companies started firing at everything that moved. Two German soldiers were killed in the street and a dozen more threw down their weapons and came out with their hands up. I was beside a building at the end of the street. G Company soldiers took charge of the prisoners and began searching all of the houses to be sure there was no one else. Suddenly I heard a motor start. A German soldier came riding out from behind a building on a motorcycle. He was burning rubber, trying to get away. I sprayed him with my Tommy gun and shot him off of the cycle. He laid it over and it went sliding across the street on its side. The rider did a few rolls and slid into a building. He never moved. He was dead. When I heard the 'all-clear' from G Company soldiers, I went over and took the cycle out of gear and took charge of it.

We waited a while for further orders and for the prisoners of war to be picked up. Word got around that we were going to be relieved by another battalion. Soon the trucks brought them up to the village. They unloaded and our battalion loaded into the trucks. The convoy turned around and went down the crooked mountain road that we had just come up. I started the motorcycle and rode it in the convoy down the mountain road. I had a bicycle when I was 10 years old, but I had never ridden a motorcycle before. The trucks took us to a nice level place at the bottom of the mountain by the sea. We made camp next to the blacktop highway that led to Palermo. On the other side of the road was the beach. In a couple of days the fighting was over. They said the campaign had taken 38 days. I would have to take their word for that. It was hard to keep up with days of the week. Everyone wanted to ride the motorcycle. We used it to deliver messages to other companies and battalion headquarters. The motorcycle did cause a few minor injuries. One guy misjudged a hairpin curve up on the mountain and went over the side of the road. He and the cycle landed in a clump of bushes about 10 feet below the road. He was scratched up a little. He looked like he had been fighting a tiger but it was nothing serious. The bike was fine. Some soldiers helped him get it back on the road, and he rode it back to camp.

While we were there, Bob Hope and Frances Langford, and company came and performed a U.S.O. Show. The engineers built a platform at the bottom of a small hill. It was like an amphitheater. Everyone sat on the side of the knoll a little above the platform. It was a really good show. They will always be special people to me. For two hours they made me forget what had been happening those 38 days. Bob Hope reminded us of what we were fighting to defend: Mom, Dad, our country, and apple pie.

Bob Hope & Frances Langford

One day, six of us from my platoon went across the road and went swimming. One of the six was Bob DeAngelo. He was an American-born Italian and spoke the Italian language fluently. Bob acted as our interpreter and we learned a few Italian phrases from him. On the way to the beach we met a small Italian boy. I would guess he was about 8 or 10 years old. Bob told the boy in Italian that we were going swimming and the boy said that he wanted to go with us. When we arrived at the beach we went far enough out that the water was just over our heads. We were playing keep-away with a piece of driftwood when after a few minutes, we happened to look towards the beach and found that it was at the very least half a mile away. The soldiers on the beach and the jeeps traveling on the highway looked like tiny toys or ants. We had drifted out, pulled by an under-current. None of us panicked and we began to swim toward the shore. We swam steadily without stopping and were about halfway to the shore when the little Italian boy gave out. He just quit swimming and started to sink under the water. I was swimming the backstroke beside him and reached out and caught him before he sank out of sight. We all took turns pulling him along. It took over two hours swimming against the tide before we were able to reach the beach. By the time we got to the shore we were all so tired that we just staggered up onto the sand and fell face downward. We were there for several minutes before anyone could move. I had never heard of a rip-tide before but every time I told anyone about our experience, they said that they knew all about them. Some had heard of people being carried away and lost at sea. Well, I believe we came real close to being lost ourselves. The young boy showed more emotion than anyone else did. He thanked us over and over in his native language. The little fellow was brave and showed lots of courage throughout the whole ordeal. I knew that we were very lucky that we made it safely to shore.

We stayed in the camp by the beach for 22 days resting from the long walk across Sicily. We replaced our lost equipment, and by that time I had learned that I could get along fine without some of the equipment assigned to us such as my shelter half, mess kit, tent stakes, and extra clothing. I always carried ammunition, my weapon, one blanket, a canteen, a canteen cup, the clothes that I had on, a little shovel and a backpack to carry K-rations and hand grenades in. This was all I needed. It made the load that I carried a lot lighter. The woolen uniform was enough to keep me warm from the cool sea breeze at night. At least until winter.

A Summary of the Campaign in Sicily

The German and Italian armies who were defeated in Africa in the early part of 1943 were led by Erwin Rommell, the great German general known as the Desert Fox by the allied forces, who were led by British General Montgomery and American General Patton.

The German army tried to take all the men and equipment it could and escape to Italy, Sicily, and southern France. It was decided that Sicily would be a logical springboard for the Allied invasion of Italy and the continent of Europe.

114

Allied land forces in this campaign were comprised of the U.S. 7th Army under General George Patton and the British 8th Army under General Montgomery. Troops totaling 160,000 Americans, British, Canadians, and French were assembled and made ready to invade the island. The Axis force was estimated to be 200,000. They consisted of nine divisions of the Italian 6th Army, two German armored divisions, and two motorized infantry divisions.

The Allied air force bombed Axis bases in Sicily and ships in the Mediterranean Sea during June and July of 1943 ending on the nights of July 9th and 10th with large-scale air attacks on airfields and on areas where landing craft and paratroops would attack. Assault troops began moving in shortly after midnight. The navy bombarded enemy coastal artillery batteries and areas where large numbers of enemy troops were gathered. By 6:00 a.m. on the morning of July 10th, all landings were reported successful. By the end of the day, Ally and army beachheads were firmly established from 4 to 10 miles deep. The following day they continued inward to their respective objectives against a confused and disorganized enemy army.

After many unsuccessful counterattacks by the German and Italian armies and some fierce fighting in August, the campaign was over in 38 days. The Axis forces began their final withdrawal from Sicily in the mountainous terrain in the northeast part of the island. At a point near Mount Etna and only two miles across the strait from the southern tip of the Italian "boot", protected by coast defenses and anti-aircraft guns, the Axis forces were able to evacuate more than three German divisions and many Italian divisions to the mainland of Italy.

American casualties included 1425 killed, 5200 wounded and 791 missing in action. British casualties were estimated at 9353. The Sicilian campaign cost the Axis over 164,900 men; 32,100 of them were Germans. They lost 70 tanks, 282 heavy artillery guns, 3,500 motor vehicles, many aircraft, and ONE MOTORCYCLE!

CHAPTER 15
SALERNO - War on the Mainland

On September 8th, 1943, we were told to break camp. We were assembled and briefed and told that we would be attacking the mainland of Italy. It would be another amphibious landing. We would be told where we would land after we were at sea.

We were taken to Palermo by truck convoy. John Price rode the motorcycle alongside the jeeps and trucks. We boarded a ship and set sail that evening. Just before midnight on September 9th, we disembarked over the side of the ship. We were to hit the beach just south of Salerno, Italy, at 4:00 a.m. This was a safe landing for us. The 3rd and 36th divisions had landed there in the early morning hours of September 9th and had met stiff opposition from the German army. They had fought their way inland, driving the enemy to the foothills of the mountains. The Germans had retreated to the other side of the Salerno River. Both divisions had many casualties.

Our objective was a bridge over the Salerno River. We were to follow the dirt road to the river twenty-five miles inland, then spread out along the river and try to prevent the Germans from blowing the bridge. As we came around the end of a little mountain ridge, we could see the bridge across a maize field about a quarter of a mile away. The Germans were waiting for us on the other side of the river. They opened fire on us with artillery and 88-millimeter tank shells. I could hear the screaming of the artillery shells. We scattered to the left of the road into a maize field about waist high. To the right was a steep slope led up to the hogback ridge. The officers and drivers left their jeeps and dove into the maize with us. They also left our big supply truck which was loaded with water and K-Rations. We crawled through the maize toward the river bottom about 200 yards away. There were thick trees and underbrush along the riverbank. We regrouped in the brush by the river but I did not see any of the officers again until late that evening.

Along with several of the men in my platoon, I crawled through the underbrush to where we could see the bridge. It had not been blown up yet. I guessed that the Germans thought that they might use it again themselves. We could also see some tanks and big artillery pieces partly camouflaged. They had not fired at us for several minutes. I fired at several targets with my Tommy gun; and the whole platoon joined in with their rifles. Suddenly an enemy tank shell hit a tree nearby. It was a range finder. We had been discovered and over-matched. We scattered and took cover in the tall trees just in time. Here came another barrage. For the next 5 minutes, artillery and tank shells burst all around us.

About noon, a sergeant from E Company came through the bushes and found us. He said that his company had scattered also and that he had been sent to tell everyone he saw that we were supposed to gather about 5 miles back and regroup. He said the two companies following us turned back before the enemy ever saw them and they were digging in back there.

We were out of water and rations. Since there was plenty of both on the truck up on the road, I decided that we should try to go get some. I told the platoon to stay there. Louis Rouston and I went through the maize patch back to the truck. The Germans must have expected us to do that. As we reached the road, I heard the big artillery guns fire and the screaming of the shells high in the air. Louie and I ran back toward the river through the maize. We left the truck just in time as they hit the area for 5 minutes. The truck and jeeps were destroyed and we did not have time to get any K rations or water. I decided it was time to get back to our company.

By then it was midday and hot and humid. On the way back, we stayed in the brush along the river out of sight of the enemy and soon found our battalion. Back in 1939 when I first joined the National Guard some of the old-timers in the company told us new recruits that the American army never retreats. Call it what you like: withdraw, pull back, retreat. Well, we retreated that day, and it would not be the last time. I did not mind moving back, digging in, and regrouping. The Germans caught us in a trap, a "no-win" situation for us. They say, "Discretion is the better part of valor", and I believe it was for us that day. The enemy stayed on the other side of the Salerno River. That left about 5 miles between them and us, at least for the time being. When I reached the assembly area, my Captain told me to take his jeep and driver back to the beach and bring back a load of K-rations and water.

We found huge stacks of water and rations by the sea. The ships were still anchored about half a mile out. The personal boats that brought us ashore were bringing the supplies from the ships and unloading them on the beach. While we were loading the supplies on the jeep, we heard a loud explosion coming from the area where the ships were anchored. A small cloud of white smoke was drifting toward us. Some of the quartermaster men who were unloading and stacking supplies yelled, "GAS!" That was as close to panic as I ever want to see. My mind flashed back to the old World War I vets in Lindsay, Oklahoma, who had respiratory problems from breathing the poison gas in France. Those stories about poison gas and hand-to-hand combat with the enemy always bothered me more than anything else did.

The quartermaster men were running toward a huge stack of gas masks. We followed them and quickly put on a gas mask. Before we finished loading our jeep with supplies, word came from one of the workers that someone on the ship had accidentally set off a tear gas grenade. We finished our loading and tried to remember what the beach looked like in the dark that morning before daylight. We could see the place where we came ashore where our boat stopped on the sandbar and we stepped off the ramp into waist-deep water and waded ashore.

When we arrived at our company location, we distributed the water and rations to the men. My platoon leader, Lieutenant Necuda, had already spread the platoon out and had them to dig in. Louie and I found us a spot and dug our foxhole. It would be our refuge for several days. The German artillery pounded us continually. The Germans had observers in the mountains. Every time we moved in the daytime, we received a barrage of artillery fire. So we waited until dark to distribute rations and water and stretch our legs. Our big guns were firing back at them and our planes bombed them daily.

We were in the bottomland from the edge of the mountain to the Salerno River. The 3rd division was to our right. They had moved up into the mountains by following a narrow, crooked road. At the top of the peak, the road ran through a narrow pass. One of the 3rd division companies approached the pass and began to check it out. The entire pass was lined with two and three-story stone houses. The people had moved out and left the area. The houses all faced each other, and they were so close together that the pass was only wide enough for one vehicle to go through at a time. There was no room for vehicles to pass each other.

The men from the 3rd division saw a battalion of German tanks approaching the pass from the other side. The company commander told his men to spread out and take cover in places where the tank crews could not see them. A young squad leader by the name of Audie Murphy crawled to the top of the pass to get a better view. Audie climbed over the top of one of the houses to a little porch on the second story of the house that stuck out over the pass. He positioned himself so that when the tanks moved through, they would be directly under him. When the first tank moved through the pass and came directly under Audie, he dropped a hand grenade into the turret, killing the crew and permanently disabling the tank. Because of the brave action of Audie Murphy, the tank convoy had to back up, turn around, and go back down the mountain. There was no other way through the mountains except by the river valley where we had dug in.

Murphy received the Silver Star for his bravery and forethought that day. This was only one of many medals he would receive before the war was over, including the Congressional Medal of Honor. Audie Murphy is my hero and he always will be, for I believe he saved my life that day and not only my life but he also may have saved both the 45th and the 3rd divisions. If that group of German tanks had made it through the pass and come down the mountain road, they would have come out behind our front line between the sea and us. We would have been surrounded. Our supply lines would have been cut off. Our communications would have been destroyed and our supplies on the beach captured. We had read in the *Stars and Stripes* that one of Hitler's favorite statements was that he would drive the Allied Army into the sea. How close he came that day we will never know.

We spent several more days in our foxholes, firing our weapons at anything that moved in front of us. There were some partially destroyed houses in front of us that the enemy was using. Machine guns, mortars, tanks, and artillery continually fired on us. One morning, the shooting stopped. The silence was wonderful. We fired a few rounds but there was no answering fire. We were still cautious when we started coming out and moving around, but it was for real. The Germans had pulled out. We heard that the 3rd division had fought their way over the mountain and made a counterattack on the Nazi army in front of us. We in the lower ranks did not always hear or know about a lot of the big-time maneuvers but we were grateful for what happened and glad to get out of that hole.

I did not realize then that the next month or more we would be chasing the Germans as we did in Sicily. They would be setting up roadblocks at every convenient place, trying to catch us unaware to slow our advance. They would set up a defense for a day or two and then move out. The chase would be on as soon as they left. They also ravaged and destroyed every town and village before they moved on and left them.

Even if the trees or hills hid the villages from our view before we reached them, we still knew they were there. We could smell them from a long way off. They did not have sewage systems so they used canyons and ravines for their waste disposal. Almost every village was vacated when we arrived and the buildings had been shelled or bombed. The people would return when we captured their village and tell us how grateful they were and how badly the Germans had treated them. It always made me think how awful it must be to be treated that way in their own country. I also never wanted the United States to be overrun like that, so it made me feel real good to be there, doing what I could to prevent that from happening. I never regretted any of it. I still don't, and I was so proud to be there. I did not do anything outstanding. I just took orders and did my best to carry them out. I was just as scared as the other guys but we all tried not to let the other guys know. We never knew what was going to happen from one day to the next or from one minute to the next. My idea was to take it one thing at a time and do the best I could do in each situation.

What we did not know at that time was that the Germans were building a defense line all the way across Italy, through the mountains about halfway between Naples and Rome, through Monte Cassino. They even used the monastery as a refuge during the months to follow. They built cement bunkers, all kinds of stone walls, trenches, roads, camouflaged areas, and everything else they could use to stop the Allied advance. They were trying to slow us down any way they could so they would have more time to build their defense while we were chasing the German army up the deadly "boot". We would catch up with them now and then so we had to be forever careful not to fall for traps or be caught out in the open by a sniper.

I never knew my Dad to write a letter before, to me or to anyone, but one day I received a letter from him. I was almost afraid to open it because I thought it was bad news. When I did open it, I was surprised to learn that Dad and Mom had a chance to buy a 160-acre farm half a mile north of Lindsay. They did not have the money for the down payment so Dad wanted to know if they could borrow the money which I had been allotting to him each month since I had been in the army. It was in my bank account there in Lindsay. He said it was enough to make the down payment on the farm. I was so excited that Dad and Mom could finally own their own farm after being sharecroppers all these years. There was no time to waste. I told my commanding officer about the letter and got permission to go back to headquarters and send a V-Mail letter. It simply stated, "YES, YES USE ALL THE MONEY". I was so thrilled that my army pay, which Dad had been keeping for me, would be used for such a worthy cause. The V-Mail arrived in time and Dad made the purchase.

When I returned to my company that day, the captain told me that I was being considered for a field promotion to 2nd lieutenant. A platoon officer in one of the rifle companies had been badly wounded and they were going to fill the vacancy with one of six candidates. Four of them had already been eliminated so it was down to either that platoon's sergeant or me.

The captain told me the next day that the other sergeant had been commissioned. I had mixed emotions about that. I was looking forward to the challenge and I would have welcomed the extra responsibility, but I thought they made the right choice. It would not have been fair to promote me over that sergeant who had done a good job leading those men; men he knew personally. In fact, I think it would have been a big mistake to put me in that position. Sometimes the army did things that I did not agree with, but this was not one of them. I had already learned that if something happened that was not exactly what I liked, I should forget about it and go on with what I was already doing.

The Germans continued their "cat and mouse" game with us. We sent patrols up ahead each night. Half of the company slept while the rest stood guard. They changed places at midnight. One morning, the captain sent a messenger to tell all platoon sergeants to report to company headquarters for a briefing on the orders of the day. Two other sergeants and myself were walking across an open field on our way to the command post when we heard a boom, and then the scream of a mortar shell. The usual reaction, if you were not in a foxhole, was to dive to the ground, face down. The two guys with me hit the ground. But I heard another explosion directly overhead. I had never heard a mortar shell explode in the air before. They usually exploded when they hit the ground or another object. Because it was unusual, I looked up. The shell had exploded about 200 feet above us. At least 100 pieces of white phosphorus had been blown in all directions. Each one left a trail of white smoke. As each stream of smoke turned toward the ground, the sky looked like someone had set off a Fourth of July rocket. Instead of diving to the prone position like the other two, I began to dance back and forth and side to side, dodging the falling phosphorous. By the time they all hit the ground, another incoming shell exploded overhead. The shelling lasted at least five minutes. In the end, I had managed to dodge all of it. I must have looked like an outfielder trying to catch a high fly ball on a windy day, except I was trying n□□to catch any. I heard the two sergeants yelling and jumping around on the ground. When it was over I looked after them. They both got several burns on their back, legs and arms and they had to go to the medics. This was just another way the Germans made life miserable for us. A grass pasture, a haystack, and a trash dump had caught on fire. We could see old Mt. Vesuvius to the west. I knew that the ruins of the ancient city of Pompeii lay at the foot of that mountain. Smoke was rising from her top. Something had set it off and it spewed hot lava down her sides for the remainder of the fall and winter. Maybe the exploding of the big shells had caused the eruption.

The Germans had another way to make life miserable. It was a six-barrel mortar. It fired six shells, in rapid fire, one after the other. The shells landed and exploded in a straight line about 20 feet apart. The screaming and rapid explosions were deafening and mighty scary.

B Company captured one of the mortars. The barrels were mounted on a wheel. Each one was a little longer than the next one was. This accounted for the distance between where the shells fell. When the barrels were all loaded they rotated the wheel causing each barrel to pass by a single firing pin. All shells were dangerous and nerve-racking. But that six-barrel job had a terrifying sound. They used it a lot at night to keep us awake and do what damage they could.

We were in the mountains somewhere east of Naples. From the mountains, we could see a small village up ahead. Our artillery had shelled it with many shells that morning while the Germans were still there. Not much was left but ruins. When we tried to enter after running the Germans out, the Germans hit the village with a barrage of shells. There were craters everywhere, six to eight feet across and four to six feet deep. While we were entering the village we heard the roar of an airplane coming in fast. It was low and coming from between two ridges. By the time it came in sight, everyone knew it was a German Luftwaffe plane. Pandemonium set in. Everyone was yelling, "Get down! Airplane! Hit the dirt!" and so on. People were running in all directions. I was running for the nearest crater. It seemed that everyone had the same idea. Before I could reach the crater, the plane started strafing. The last few feet I dove and went airborne toward the crater. When I landed, the crater was level full of people. I landed on top of the pile. My body was at ground level. My head was close to the edge of the hole. The rapid fire of the bullets kicked up a straight line of dust as they whizzed by about six inches in front of my face. The plane passed directly over us, so low I thought it was going to touch the ground. The roar was deafening. It was all over instantly. I got up and one by one, the rest of the guys got out of the crater. There were ten of us in all in that one hole. I told them I was sorry for piling on. They said they did not mind a bit. I could shield them with my body any time I wanted to.

We moved on as fast as it was safe to move, but very cautiously. We were only a few miles away when Naples fell. The Germans almost completely demolished it before leaving. They even sank several ships in the harbor. Then they bombed and strafed and shelled it after they left. The next really tough defense the enemy made was at the Volturno River. They set their defense on the north side of the river and we moved up on the south side. It was another battle of the artillery. They shelled us constantly, and we did it to them. The 36th division dug in along the river where it was deep. They had many casualties trying to cross the river in boats, on rafts, and by wading.

While we were there, our 1st sergeant got sick and was sent back to a hospital in North Africa. The captain told me to take over his duties. I was 1st sergeant for a few days, but before he could make it official, I was shot though the right wrist, and it got infected. I went to the aid station with a fever of 102 degrees. They sent me to a field hospital in the rear near Salerno. It was a huge tobacco drying building. It was about the size of an average gymnasium with a high ceiling. It was open on all sides and was still full of tobacco hanging from the top.

Thanks to penicillin they were able to stop the infection and fever and the wound healed. I returned to the front in about ten days. When I caught up with my company they had fought their way across the Volturno River and were in pursuit of the enemy again. The captain had promoted another guy to 1st sergeant, but he had not filled my position. I had missed another promotion, but I did not care much. I liked the guys in my platoon and liked what I was doing. I had the best platoon in the whole army. My mom used to say, "Don't cry over spilled milk". And my dad would say, "Don't worry about something you can't do anything about." Those two bits of advice have always meant a lot to me. So I got on with doing my job as a platoon sergeant.

We camped one night near a small town. I don't remember the names of any of those villages. There were no signs, and I could not pronounce them anyway. This little village had been flattened by artillery, except for a beautiful monastery at the edge of town. It had not been touched. I took a squad and went to the monastery to check it out. That was the most beautiful building I had ever seen. There were life-size paintings and statues along every wall in the sanctuary, in the halls, and behind the altar. The second story was all small rooms. They were the monks' private bedrooms.

The next day we moved real fast. The enemy had withdrawn to a mountain range ahead. We marched for about three hours after dark fell that night. We made camp by the side of the road. Lieutenant Baldwin sent for me to come to his tent. He told me to take his jeep and driver and three other men and continue along the road about three or four miles. He said the road would come to a canyon, bear left half a mile along the canyon, and come to a bridge. He wanted to know if the Germans had blown the bridge and if we could see any signs of the enemy on the other side of the canyon. He cautioned me to run the jeep in low gear at idle speed and to have the men be as quiet as possible. (As if we were going to sing "100 Bottles of Beer on the Wall!") He said that if I encountered any Germans, everybody was to get back on the jeep, turn it around and "high tail it" out of there. Now, I had been on half a dozen scouting missions, most of them at night and out in front of our front lines, but never had I taken a jeep along before. They say there is always a first time for everything!

The lieutenant had told me to report to him at his tent as soon as I got back. He said that he would be awake because he had to meet with the colonel and all of the company commanders to plan the next day's attack. I had asked for volunteers in my platoon and got a dozen. I took Huey Long, who was the driver, and three other men. It was a clear night. The moon had gone down earlier but we could see a few feet ahead because of the starlight and the jeep's blackout lights. We started out and I took the lead, walking about ten feet in front of the jeep. The others walked beside the jeep. The directions the Lieutenant gave me from his map were correct and easy to follow. We reached the canyon and followed the road to the left. We soon came to a wide gate on the left side of the road. The gate was thrown back and a large stake had been driven in the middle of the opening with a dark colored rag tied to it. I pulled the rag loose and stuffed it in my pocket. It was just a few more feet to the bridge. Both sides of the canyon had a small strip of grass and bushes. The road made a sharp turn that led onto the bridge. There was a huge tree by the bridge that was a good place to observe from. The bridge had been blown at the other end. It had fallen down into the canyon.

Huey turned the engine off. I could see tombstones in the field where I had taken the rag. It was so quiet it was scary. The canyon was about 10 feet deep and 60 feet wide. We would have to bull doze a place to cross if we took a vehicle over. From behind the tree I scanned the other side. I could not see anything unusual. But for some reason I felt that a hundred eyes were watching us from the other side. It was just too quiet. It had been my experience that I could hear noise of birds or animals at night when no one was around. I whispered, "Let's get out of here!" Huey backed the jeep into the cemetery entrance and we turned back.

When we reached camp, the lieutenant was waiting up for me. I told him that the bridge had fallen in and that it would be impossible to cross it. He said that was what the commanding officers wanted to know. I told him we did not actually see anyone, but I felt like someone was there watching us. That was the best I could do. I explained that it was too quiet. I showed him the rag I had brought back from the graveyard entrance. It was bright red, and had the letters "Achtung: Minen" printed on it which was German for "Attention: Mines".

We were awakened at daylight the next morning and moved out in attack formation. G and E Companies went through the grass and bushes in the level land beside the road that we had followed the night before. My company went up the sloping ridge to their left. We followed a narrow trail along the top of the ridge. As we climbed I could see G and E Companies making their way through the underbrush in battle formation. I saw the graveyard and the blown bridge as they passed by them.

At the very top of the long ridge we found a vacated village of six houses. The houses were nice. They appeared to be vacation homes. The only way to reach them was the trail that we had followed up the ridge. One of the houses had a big basement beneath it. We were lucky to get in the basement when the shelling started. Big artillery shells blasted the village for five or ten minutes before we realized they were coming from our own guns in the rear. The spotter for the artillery had come up the ridge where he could get a better view of the targets on the other side of the mountain. He called his battalion by radio and told them to stop the barrage, but not because he knew we were on his side! He said that the gunners were aiming too low and to try to drop the shells just on the other side of the ridge. They almost blew those six houses away before the lieutenant got word to them to shut down.

As we watched below, we saw G Company bypass the graveyard and the minefield. They started to cross an open field to get back to the canyon close to the bridge. The Germans were waiting for them on the other side of the canyon in the bushes. The Nazis fired burp guns, machine guns, mortars, and rifles. There were many casualties. We got a call on the radio that they needed help to evacuate the dead and wounded. I asked for volunteers and the whole platoon stood up and said, "Let's go!" I was so proud of them. I felt like I was ten feet tall.

The medics had been able to climb the ridge in the four-wheel drive jeeps. Along with their medical supplies, they had brought a lot of stretchers. We took them and went, under cover, down to the bottom of the mountain. We found a sergeant and the survivors of his platoon waiting for us. He said the other three platoons of G Company had moved through the woods to his left and had reached the canal. But he and his men had to cross an open field and that was when the enemy opened fire on them.

I could hear some of the wounded calling out "Help! Medics!" By peeking out of the ditch I could see some of them. I tied a dirty white handkerchief on my gun barrel and waved it back and forth above my head. In a few minutes (it seemed like a long time) a German soldier stood up on the other side of the canyon waving a white flag. I stood up real slow. I felt like I was in someone's gun sight. In fact I was pretty sure of it. I only trusted them because I had to do it. It was the only way that we could evacuate our wounded and dead. Without a word I walked out on to the open field. Every man followed me including the G Company men.

We gathered the wounded first. I helped lift them onto the stretchers to get the litter bearers back off of the field. Then we picked up the dead. I kept looking all over the field to make sure we did not miss anyone. Finally I saw someone lying behind a log at the edge of the clearing. He was a young lad, about 16 years old, that had been shot in the foot. It was a real bad wound that had bled a lot. He told me he had been watching us carry the others out while he tied a strip of his shirt around his foot to stop the bleeding. He waited for us to carry the others out because he thought their wounds were worse than his were. I thought that was the bravest thing a soldier could do. I was satisfied that there was no one else. I knelt down in front of him so he could get on my back. I stood up and carried him piggyback up the mountain following the others. As I left the field, I took one more glance all around to see if that was everyone. As I stepped down into the ditch, I turned and waved one arm high above my head. I meant for it to say, "Thanks". I hope they took it to mean that. I began to climb the steep slope of the hogback ridge. The trail of the litter bearers was easy to follow. I have often wished that I could remember that young man's name that I carried up the mountain. The jeeps and half-ton ambulances carried the solders down the trail that we had used that morning and took them to the aid station.

I have thought about that day many times. Twenty-five or thirty brave men were answering the call to rescue their comrades. It was an honor and a privilege to serve with such brave men. They were like brothers to me. War brought people together that otherwise would never have met.

The Bible says "Be still and know that I am God" (Psalm 46:10) and "the righteous cry out and the Lord hears them. He delivers them from all their troubles" (Psalms 34:17). I praised God daily and thanked Him for allowing me to get through another day. I believed that the only reason that I was still alive was that my guardian angel that my dad used to tell me about was real and was with me all the time. Prayer always made me feel good. It gave me a feeling of peace and security. Ever since that night in Sicily when I prayed for God to see that I got home alive to my family, I had felt that someday, somehow I would get home alive to my mom and dad and my brothers and sisters.

Our artillery bombarded the German positions on the other side of the canyon for the next two days. Our artillery spotter had a good view from the high ridge where we were, and he did a good job directing the shots on their gun emplacements along the ditches and bushes where their men were hidden. During those two days the canyon was our front line. The enemy had so many casualties and equipment losses that they withdrew to the next mountain. We crossed the canyon and advanced until we made contact with the enemy again and dug in. The engineers came and made a bypass by the bridge. Our trucks and jeeps could get through with our rations, ammunition, and other supplies. John Price, one of the guys in my platoon, rode my Italian-looted motorcycle to bring us a message. He was pushing the bike through the bypass up the steep slope the bulldozer had made when the bike wheel ran over a mine the Germans had planted before they pulled out. John miraculously survived the explosion with only minor cuts and bruises, and his hearing was not good for a day or two. The mine did produce one casualty, though. It blew the wheel off of the motorcycle and tore the bike to pieces, so on that sad day I said goodbye to my looted motorcycle.

Down in the ranks we did not know that we had reached the famous German "Gustov" defense line. It stretched all the way across Italy from the east coast to the west coast through the most rugged mountains that we had encountered. This was the great defense line they had been building ever since we had entered Italy at Salerno. They had built concrete bunkers, gun emplacements, and observation points in well placed positions all through the highest ranges and had built roads in from the north for their supply lines. Hitler and his generals hoped to stop the Allied army from advancing any farther north in Italy than the "Gustov" line, and it worked for the next eight or nine months. The famous Monastery of World War II was in the middle of the defense line. Hitler had planned that, too. It was not only a great barricade, high up on a tall mountain peak, but he was counting heavily on the idea that the Allies would not bomb it. The Germans used it as a safe sanctuary for their troops.

This was the first time we had been in a stationary position for that long. Winter was there by that time. It was cold and wet and the nights were long and freezing up in the highlands. The Germans pounded us day and night with every kind of weapon they had;

artillery, machine guns, and mortars. Our troops attacked and counterattacked their line of bunkers and pill boxes. We were so high up that jeeps could not go all the way because of the steep and rugged trails. So they brought our rations and supplies on pack mules. One soldier would lead the first mule and the others were tied together in a line behind it. There were about a dozen pack mules in each train. T. J. Goodner, a very good friend of mine from Maysville, Oklahoma, was in charge of one of the pack mule trains.

One day I saw a group of pack mules winding their way up the side of the mountain next to us. All of the mules were black or brown except for one. That one was pretty and red and looked just like old Snip, the little red mule that Dad had raised and that I broke and rode to the schoolhouse at night when we had basketball practice. The canyon between us was too deep to go see if it was Snip, so I just put it out of my mind. I decided that Dad would never sell old Snip anyway. She was his pet and his pride and joy. He had trained her to come to him when he called her by name and to rub her nose on his face when he said, "Give me a kiss." I knew Dad would never get rid of her.

We stayed on the front through December until around January 1st. Christmas was just another day of shelling and shooting. We were relieved and we moved back and made camp east of Naples. We had hot meals, baths, and clean clothes. Several men each day, from each company, were allowed to go into Naples on a one-day pass. Trucks transported them.

While we were there, Lieutenant Carruso from the 3rd battalion came over to our camp and asked for me. He asked me if I would go with him to where they were camped. He needed help with one of his men who had drunk too much wine and who was getting out of hand. He had gotten wild and mean and had threatened to shoot up the camp. Almost all of his company had gone to Naples that day. I knew Lieutenant Carruso and he was a fine officer, a gentleman, and a brave platoon leader. I gladly said, "Yes", and went with him.

When we arrived, the soldier was staggering between the pup tents with a rifle, waving it and pointing it at tents and trees and rocks. A medic was standing by, waiting for us at the C.P. tent. All the other soldiers had either left or hidden out of sight. The lieutenant and I made our plan. We walked toward the drunken soldier. The medic followed us with a syringe and needle. As we got close to him, the lieutenant called him by name and just talked to him as if nothing was wrong. We separated and when we were even with the soldier we both ran into him at the same time. I grabbed one arm and a leg and so did the lieutenant and we threw him to the ground, taking the rifle from him as we went down. When we hit the ground the medic was there. We held the soldier down while the medic gave him a shot. He passed out shortly and slept until the next morning.

Some time later I got word that Lieutenant Carruso had been hit between the eyes by a sniper's bullet while leading his platoon on a scouting mission. He died instantly. I was saddened by that report, but I was glad to have known him. And I was proud that I got to spend that day with him corralling the inebriated soldier. On the very same day that I learned of Lt. Carruso's death, I learned that my old and dear friend, 1st Sergeant Bill Wier of my original company, Regimental Headquarters Company, 179th Infantry, had been killed by a direct hit from an artillery shell. That brought back a lot of memories of old Camp Barkley, when I was in that company with Bill and we played golf together. When something bad happened to a good friend, we just had to tighten our belts and move on, but that was a very sad day for me.

Near the end of January 1944, we were told we would be moving out real soon. We cleaned our guns, replaced our lost equipment, and I wrote an E-Mail letter to my folks. We were not allowed to give much information. Every letter was censored. But I let them know that I was well. We were told that we would get the details of our move later. We were convoyed to Naples where we boarded a ship and set sail. On February 3rd, we landed near Anzio, a small seaport about fifty miles southwest of Rome and about 200 miles behind the German lines. The good news was that the 3rd and 36th divisions landed there, too. It was a walk-on. We landed with out any opposition. General Marcus W. Clark had out smarted the great German General Kesselring and his many Panzer divisions. But they would not be down for long.

A typical shore landing
(This was taken D-Day, in France)

We crossed the beach, reorganized, and continued inland. Our area was to the northeast of Anzio, just outside of Rome. The three divisions formed a half circle from sea to sea with Anzio in the center. It was farming country, fairly level, with a few gentle slopes. A network of canals irrigated it. All the water had been drained from the canals. Just two to six inches remained from the recent rains.

There were two-story stucco houses with red tile roofs in each field. They had stables on the ground floor for the livestock. Almost all of the houses were built exactly alike except they faced in different directions. There was no definite pattern to the houses. We called the area "the factory". As in all other areas we had occupied, the people had departed to safety and took their livestock and their personal possessions with them.

The route of the 45th Division, 1944

We made camp, set up a C.P. tent, spread out, and dug foxholes by the sides of the canals that ran east and west. We posted guards and began waiting, wondering what would happen next and when it would happen.

CHAPTER 16
The Anzio Beachhead

After I joined the army, I always attended church at the chapel wherever I was stationed. But I didn't really start understanding how being a Christian affected my life until I made that first amphibious landing with my division on an enemy-occupied beach in Sicily. I soon realized that the enemy meant business, and that they meant to wipe us out in any way that they could. I made up my mind then and there that life was uncertain. And that if I did not believe there was an Almighty God, but it turned out that there was, I would be in deep trouble. So I learned to pray the night after our first battle in Sicily. I believed that my prayers would be answered, and they were. My faith grew stronger day by day, and it gave me strength and courage each day to know that God was Almighty and that He was there with me.

Patrols from our battalion were sent out. They had reached the edge of Rome and saw no enemy. On D-Day plus two, I was standing guard on the dirt road that ran through our position from Anzio. A jeep came up the road from the rear. A driver and a lieutenant were in the front seats. Two soldiers with rifles were in the back. They stopped and the officer spoke to me. He said, "Sergeant, we are going into Rome on reconnaissance." He paused and grinned and then continued, "We are going to see the Pope. We should be back in a couple of hours. Look for us and don't shoot. We may be coming back in a hurry!" With that they drove out of sight in a northerly direction, toward Rome.

They returned in about three hours and said they had been all the way to the center of Rome to a place that looked like a town square in Texas. They saw no sign of the German army.

General Marcus W. Clark did not ask us "dog-faces" if he had made the right decision when he stopped our advance and had us dig in and wait for the enemy. But, the troops and some of the officers were very unhappy that we were like sitting ducks. Many were asking why we did not take Rome and block the roads leading inward from the north and south. That would have cut the German supply line to Naples as well as the "Gustov" defense line. The idea of taking Rome made sense to me. But they were running the war, and we were just fighting it. Historians and war analysts have criticized General Clark severely for making that decision. They say it cost the American Army thousands of casualties, both dead and wounded. The huge American cemetery at Nettuno near Anzio is proof that the historians and scholars were right. The word got back to us that General Clark's excuse was that he did not want to fight a war in the Vatican City. I am no general, but that just did not make sense to me. We gave the Germans the city of Rome free of charge. They stationed their reserves where their headquarters were. More importantly, they had the high ground to the north and east of Rome. From there they could see our entire position and see all of our troop movements. They also held the railroad and highways in and out of the city.

From where I was, it was a week of unrest and uncertainty. Not knowing what was coming, when they would be there, and how many there would be. In short we had given the German army a big advantage. This was the first time we had dug in when there was no enemy in front of us.

My old company, 179th regimental headquarters company, lost a master sergeant while we were waiting for something to happen. Their captain sent for me and he offered the position to me. Without hesitation I told him I could not take the promotion. For once in my career, I had turned down a promotion. I simply did not want to transfer out of my company. Call it sentimental or whatever. It was something I could not explain then, and I cannot explain it now. I just did not want to leave those guys because I had been through so much with them and I had grown so fond of them. I knew that when the going got rough they would be there for each other. I have had no regrets about that decision. It was like a state of mind that causes us to do what we want to do. And I liked what I was doing. I was with a group of men that would do their very best at whatever they were asked to do.

The next six days were the same old routine. We had 3 weeks of rest near Naples, a boat ride to Anzio, and now this. The troops began to settle down. We even had a game of flag football each evening. Don't ask me where the football came from or how it got there, because I don't know. About D-Day plus eight, while we were playing football, a German artillery shell came screaming through the sky from the north and exploded in the field where we were playing. "Jerry" had arrived. We all hit the dirt. When the shrapnel stopped falling, we grabbed our helmets and our rifles and dashed for our foxholes. That was the beginning of a long and bloody struggle for the Anzio beachhead. That first shell was only a range finder. They followed up with a rolling barrage that lasted for an hour or so. One of my men was hit with shrapnel while he was diving for cover.

There was a house near the canal. The officers were using the stable for a command post. Our communications jeep with the big radio mounted in it was parked behind the house along with one of the officer's jeeps. The radio was on 'receive only'. We always had radio silence except in an emergency. Radio operators scanned the frequencies day and night. Operators Cpl. Frank Latch, Warren G. Howard, Bob DeAngelo, Gus Gishwatner, and Colbert W. Starr were sitting in the two jeeps listening for both American and German incoming messages. Suddenly, several 88-millimeter German tank shells hit the corner of the building, destroying the corner and blowing tons of rock and shrapnel onto the men and the jeeps. The area between the canal and the house was covered with rock. When the rocks stopped falling, I peeked over the edge of the canal. What I saw was a shocking sight. I climbed out of the trench and ran to where the jeeps were Rock, dust, and smoke was thick all around. The men were buried under rocks and tile. I immediately started throwing the rocks aside.

The first man I found was Frank Latch. I uncovered him and tried to raise him up. He called my name and mumbled something I could not understand, then went limp in my arms. I knew he was dead. I uncovered the man who had been sitting next to him. It was Warren G. Howard. He was already dead. I uncovered Bob DeAngelo. He was dead also. When I started to the other jeep, I saw Gus Gishwatner lying dead on the ground. Finally, I found Colbert W. Starr in the other jeep. As I grabbed the rocks and threw them aside, I heard him groan and yell for help. I picked him up and carried him into the stable. The colonel, the major, their staff, my company commander, his staff, and a couple of medics were all inside. They were all lying down around the wall and did not know what had happened outside. None of them were hurt. Colbert's chest and shoulder were covered with blood. I laid him down on some straw and called the medics to give me a hand. He was bleeding from a chest wound and his left arm was almost severed at the shoulder. I watched while the medics stopped the bleeding with large bandages. Then I went outside.

I went and looked at the four soldiers. They had not moved since I had found them. I felt so helpless; there was nothing I could do for them. I found some blankets and was covering them up when, all of

134

a sudden, I realized what had happened. I had lost four good friends and another one lay inside, near death. I fell on my knees right there and cried. All I could think of was that they were all good soldiers who had lost their lives fighting for their country, their homes, their families, and the American flag, the symbol of life, liberty and justice for all.

The memories of war seem to never go away. They may fade a little but they are never completely erased, especially the memories of good friends killed in battle. It seemed many times worse than a friend dying of an illness did. I guess it was because death during a battle was so sudden, and we were so excited and keyed up. Everything I did in the few minutes since the shells had hit the building, I did on impulse. All the energy I had needed was there for me. Now that I had paused for a few minutes I felt weak and sick at my stomach.

I realized that for these five guys the war was over, but it wasn't for me. There lay five of the many "heroes" of the war, the four who died, and Starr, who would go back to the states because of his injuries. All of those who gave their lives for their country were automatically heroes in my book. Those who died would never see their family and friends back home again. They would never fall in love and get married or know the blessings of having their own children and watching them grow up. They would never go to church and worship with their families. They'd never see their children and grandchildren learn, achieve, or perform in school, band, orchestra, baseball, football, basketball, soccer, or any other activities. They would never see them graduate from grade school, high school, or college. They wouldn't get the chance to lift their shoulders high with pride that not one of their children was ever in trouble with the law or ever spent any time in jail. That is what America means to me. A wonderful family that have kept their lives free of alcohol, drugs and tobacco, "the three killers." Yes, a little bit of me died that day, for the friends I had lost. I went inside to check on Starr. They had finished bandaging him, and he was awake. The bleeding had stopped. He did not try to speak, but he blinked his eyes at me. I thoughtlessly lit a cigarette and held it to his mouth, but he turned his head away. He was the only one who survived and he was soon sent home to be with his family.

I finally pulled myself together and went to check on the rest of the platoon. No one else had been injured. I told them what had happened. We found some stretchers and moved all five down the canal to the crossroad with a bridge. Someone called and arranged for ambulances to meet us there to take them to the rear.

We returned to our unit to find that the enemy was starting a counter attack aimed at our battalion. I could see a dozen Tiger tanks coming across an open field toward us. The tanks were about 40 yards apart with infantry walking in between. Everything was in a state of confusion. I got orders to alert everyone to move down the canal to the next ditch that ran to the rear and dig in at the next lateral ditch. The main canals were about 8 feet deep and 10 feet wide. When the Germans reached the canal that we had just left, they could not cross it with their tanks. The banks were too steep. By then, our Artillery spotters had called in the coordinates and our guns were shelling them. We had our infantry and artillery fighting their infantry and tanks. When our artillery zeroed in on them, they backed off. We took a few shots at them with rifles, but I couldn't tell if I hit anything or anyone. When I shot at an enemy and saw him dive to the ground, I did not know whether I hit him, just came close enough to him to scare him, or if he just decided to take a dive. This brought back memories of when I was a kid back in Lindsay, Oklahoma, listening to the four old World War I veterans telling me about fighting in the trenches in France. At that time I really didn't believe them, but here I was in a similar situation. I wondered if anyone would believe my stories when I told about this.

When we reached the canal that we were ordered to go to, we found our battalion commander standing in the middle of the canal, in water halfway up to his knees. He told me that E Company had been trapped by the advancing German tanks and infantry and had to cross an open field to escape and that they had suffered several casualties. He told me to get some of my men together and go help them evacuate the wounded. I got a group of volunteers. We found some stretchers stacked by the side of the canal and took off, up the connecting canal. Soon the canal was only about four feet deep. Then, only knee deep. We started crawling. Here came six E Company men, each pair carrying a wounded companion sidesaddle between them. They pointed to where the others were. They told us they needed the stretchers we had brought to carry the others. The ditch ended there, so we got to our feet and went across the open field to where they were. Once again I found myself in "no man's land" with no place to hide. It was not a good feeling, but it was the only way we could get to them. A corporal was waiting with the wounded. Thank God none were dead. We picked up the remaining wounded and went back the way we came, to the little ditch that got deeper as we approached the big canal. Our artillery barrage had kept the enemy pinned down while we were out there and they could not fire on us. Thank God for the artillery.

I stationed half of what was left of my platoon all along the canal. The first watch was from sundown until midnight. I took the last shift from midnight until dawn with the rest of the men. I lay down, but I did not sleep. I remember praying for a long time. I went over the things that happened that day. IT WAS SO HARD TO CONCENTRATE. The Germans fired a tank shell at us every few minutes. They whizzed over our heads, landed and exploded back close to the beach. We learned to tell artillery shells from tank shells back in Sicily. Artillery shells are lobbed high in the air. You can hear the gun go off, then you can hear the shell screaming through the air, then you can hear the shell explode. A tank shell is fired almost at ground level. The shell gets to it target before you can hear gunshot. Since the shell hit the target and exploded before you heard it coming, there is no chance to take cover from an oncoming tank shell. You have to be mighty sleepy to sleep through a tank barrage. They sounded like rolling thunder during an Oklahoma hailstorm. They were trying to keep us awake and it was working.

Soon after we relieved the guard at midnight, I began to hear big engines in enemy territory. They sounded like they were carrying a heavy load. They would idle for a short time then load up again. It sounded like there were three or four of them. It didn't take long to realize they were building dams across the canal so they could get their tanks across. We also knew that they would attack at daylight. I walked into the C. P. tent, a blackout tent we had erected that evening and sandbagged for a command post. The officer on duty nodded to me and said he heard them also.

He told me that our artillery spotter had their range from the evening before and planned to wait until the Germans started their attack in the morning and got into the open field. Then he would call for an artillery barrage on them. It sounded like a real good plan to me.

At daybreak we began to hear the sharp chatter of the German tank engines starting up. Soon after, we saw a giant army moving toward us. There were Tiger tanks about 30 or 40 yards apart as far left and right as you could see, and foot soldiers almost shoulder to shoulder. Our artillery started firing a rolling barrage right on target just like the lieutenant said they would. Our antitank guns and our

30-caliber and 50-caliber machines also opened fire. I was lying on the side of the canal peeking over the top and saw it all. I began firing away with my M-1 rifle. I had left my Thompson submachine gun in our kitchen truck back on the beach. It did not have a long enough range for this type of warfare on level ground. I still could not tell if I hit anyone, but every time I fired at an enemy they went down. Whether they were hit or I just came close and scared them, I do not know. Soon the dust from the exploding antitank and artillery shells was so thick I could not see the tanks or the enemy soldiers. Then the shelling stopped, the dust settled and the Germans had turned back to the canal they had come from. Within an hour they came again. Once more we were able to turn them back. Around noon they attacked again. This time they were able to take shelter in the shell craters. They kept coming, rushing from one shell hole to another. We were out-numbered maybe five to one or more. History tells us that the Germans had over one hundred thousand troops surrounding the beachhead. By mid-afternoon they were almost to our trench. We were ordered to move out. That old, unused word "retreat" came up again. We moved down the connecting canal to the next crossing canal. We each dug out a place in the side of the canal large enough to stand in or sit down. We also dug out another place for the blackout tent, deep enough to get it below ground level. We then sandbagged it around the inside walls.

I was exhausted, as everyone else seemed to be, as well. As I look back on that day, I am reminded that we were not the only ones dealing with situations like that. We did not have a corner on the war. Thousands and thousands of GIs on the beachhead, on the "Gustov" line north of Naples, and in the islands of the South Pacific were having similar problems. These were definitely our workdays so far. I lay down in my little dugout and tried to sleep. The exploding tank shells, the shrapnel, the dust, the whizzing bullets, and the thundering of shells as they passed overhead made it hard to rest, but I finally dozed off. The corporal of the first watch awakened me at midnight.

The Germans had several guns that were better than our American guns. They were used for the same purpose. Their burp gun was one. It fired so fast it sounded like a burp. The six-barrel mortar not only was deadly, but it was terrorizing. The Tiger tank with its 88-millimeter cannon was much better than our Sherman Tank. The Tiger Tank had much thicker walls, was much heavier and faster, and had more maneuverability. They had a 280-millimeter cannon that was so big that it took two flatbed railroad cars to transport it .The shells that it fired weighed 561 pounds. They had moved two of these big guns into Rome. That night they began firing them over the beachhead. Their range was some 55 miles with

"Anzio Annie" after being captured

enough explosives in each shell to blow a small village away. We immediately named them "*The Anzio Express*" and "*Anzio Annie*". They lobbed the shells over our heads and onto the beach and into the ship channel. These two big guns kept our ships from docking at Anzio Harbor for days and their sound was another terrorizing blow to our morale. The freight train-like sounds kept us awake day and night.

I remember being terribly sleepy that morning. But I got up and followed the corporal who awakened me to his post and relieved him. It was a clear night. The moon had gone down, but the stars shone bright enough that I could see well enough to get around. My assignment was to stand guard outside the command post blackout tent that we had pitched and sandbagged the night before. Things seemed about the same as they were the two nights before. The enemy fired the 88-millimeter tank shells close over our heads every few minutes. They exploded somewhere in the rear near the beach. I learned later that one of the shells hit the tent of the hospital where I would be taken later that very night. Several people, including one of the nurses, were wounded. I could hear the Caterpillars at work, building levies across the canal. This meant the Germans would attack again at daybreak.

Colonel Darby, Major Sturdavant, and all five of the company commanders were having a meeting inside the blackout tent. They were making plans for our defense against the coming attack. About that time the "*Anzio Express*" fired a round. The blast was so loud that it sounded like it was nearby, although it was somewhere in the rail yards of Rome, 15 miles away. The big shell screamed high overhead and landed behind us on the beach near Anzio or Nettuno about 25 miles away from our location. The tank guns continued to fire a shot about every ten minutes, and the big railroad guns fired about every hour all through the night.

There was a large shade-tree up on the bank of the canal about twenty feet from my post. I had been on duty about an hour when an 88-millimeter shell hit the tree and exploded sending shrapnel flying in all directions. Several pieces hit me in the right side of my chest near the fourth rib. The impact from the pieces of steel knocked me to the ground. I did not hear the shell coming until it exploded. It felt like a mule had kicked me in the side. Then my lung began to burn as if someone had thrust a red-hot iron into my side. I tried to get up, but I was not stable enough to stand. I crawled to the tent flap and announced that I had been hit. I remember Major Sturdavant and Lieutenant Baldwin coming to my rescue. They grabbed me under the arms and dragged me into the blackout tent. They set me up with my left shoulder leaning against the sandbags. They began ripping my shirt and undershirt off. I could see the other officers from where I sat. The colonel called the aid station by the field telephone and announced that he needed a stretcher and four men to carry me. The rest of the officers were quiet. I could not see the wound because it was too far to the back. But I could see the blood, and my chest felt like it was on fire. The major and the lieutenant immediately put two large bandages over the wound and tied them tight around my chest with the long gauze strings that came with them. The bleeding seemed to be stopped. The officers went back to their meeting and left me sitting up against the sandbags. The aid station was about two miles back, so it was a long wait. There was no wound in the front side so I knew that the scrap iron was still in my chest. I never got to thank the officers for taking care of me.

In a few minutes I realized that I did not hurt anymore. Then I began to slide sideways onto the sandbags. I slid all the way over and my face hit the dirt floor. I tried to catch myself with my hands, but for some reason they would not move. I tried to call for help but I could not make a sound. I could see two of the officers from where I lay, but they had no idea what had happened to me. I tried to square my legs around straight with my body, but they had no feeling in them and they would not move. I could see and I could hear the men talking, but I still could not make a sound come from my mouth. I remember thinking that I should not panic. Help would be there soon and I needed to stay calm and cool like my buddies and I had talked about many times.

The four medics arrived and they lost no time rolling me onto the stretcher. Without a word they started down the canal. I could hear them splashing in the ankle-deep mud and water. I could only see the stars, the high banks of the canal, and the two young men carrying the front of the stretcher. No one said anything. I remember seeing an arm lying across my chest just under my chin. It puzzled me and I thought for a few moments that it was someone else's arm. Finally, I rolled my eyes enough to see that it was my own arm draped over me and dangling off the stretcher. There was nothing I could do except let it hang. There was no feeling in my arm or my hand and I could not move it.

They carried me a long time, probably halfway to the aid station. They then came to a slope leading out of the canal. They carried me out on top to an open field and lowered me to the ground to take a break. I could tell they were exhausted because the two men in the front stepped back and squatted down to rest better. In a few minutes they stood up to continue their journey and one young man that I could not see, spoke out from behind me, saying "We may as well leave him here. He is dead. He has not moved since we started carrying him." Once again, I tried to cry out. But nothing came out of my mouth. All I could think about was that the German army would be moving this way at daybreak. There was a long silence. Long enough for me to say a silent prayer. I prayed "God, don't let them leave me here". I had barely finished that prayer when one of the young aid men said with a strong voice, "Let's take him on to the aid station and let the lieutenant decide". I breathed a sigh of relief. An angel was standing by and caused that young man to speak up for me. I have no other answer for it. They picked me up without another word and carried me to the aid station, which was a small tent at the edge of a wooded area. They laid me on the ground and called the lieutenant. I saw his hand move to untie the bandage strings and I could see the glow of a small flashlight. He quickly re-tied the bandages pulling them tight. He took my vital signs, paused, then called his ambulance driver and told the guys to load me in the ambulance. He then told the driver to get me to the field hospital as fast as he could. The ambulance was a little half-ton with no windows in the back. They slid me in on the stretcher and off we went. I still remember that ride very well. We bumped and twisted and turned and slowed down and sped up. Finally, we arrived at the tent hospital on the beach near Anzio at daybreak.

Two men and two women were waiting when the driver opened the back door. They carried me through a large tent flap into what was the operating tent and laid me on a table. The two men were doctors and were dressed in green shirts, pants, and caps. I could see them scrubbing up while the nurses were getting me ready for surgery. They asked me several questions about how I got hit, what company I was in, and who my company commander was. They seemed very disgusted with me because I did not answer them. I could not even say I was sorry or shake my head or communicate with them in any way. One nurse stuck a needle in my arm and attached a large syringe filled with liquid to it. Then she snipped off one side of my handlebar mustache. I can only guess that she did it because she was mad that I did not talk to them. When the doctors came to the table and said they were ready; the nurse told me she was going to give me sodium pentothal. I had never heard of that before. She told me to count backwards from a hundred. I counted silently. I saw her tap the syringe and the next thing I remember, I woke up on a cot in a huge barracks-type tent.

When I woke, I was bandaged all the way around my chest from my armpits to my hips. The cots were almost all filled with soldiers. All of them wore bandages on some part of their bodies.

I realized then that I was able to turn my head. I moved my arms and legs and wiggled my hands and feet. I was so happy. I called out to the nurse on duty. Her first words were, "So you finally decided to talk?" I told her that, before, I was unable to talk or move my arms or legs, or even feel anything, but that everything seemed to be working now. She said she would get the doctor to come. He would want to know about this. This was at sundown. I had been in surgery about 14 hours.

When the doctor came, he said it was a difficult operation, but he assured me that I would be all right. He said he removed a huge blood clot from my lung and took out four pieces of shell fragments of various sizes. He asked me if I would like to have them. I told him, "No." He said that my right lung was almost cut in half. He cut off the bottom half and removed it.

I asked the doctor why I had been numb and could not talk or move my arms and legs the night I was injured. He told me the blood clot had probably pinched a nerve in my spine and caused the problem. Since he had no other explanation and neither did I, I accepted his theory.

The doctor also told me that my fourth rib was shattered. He said that he removed it by cutting it off at the breastbone and at the backbone. He told me that he had sewn the membrane that is wrapped around each rib back in place and then he said, "You will grow the rib back." I did not really believe him, but I did not comment about that. I just took a wait-and-see attitude, and always kept it in mind. In the next years I found that it did grow back partially but with an unusual shape. Since then, doctors always comment about it when they see my chest x-rays.

I do not remember very much of the next eight days. What I do remember is the constant screaming of the large enemy shells as they sailed overhead or nearby and the explosions when they hit. The nurse told me that the ones from the big guns were landing in the ship channel and keeping our supply ships from entering the Anzio Harbor. The hospital was overcrowded but the ships could not come into the harbor to evacuate the wounded.

On my eighth day in the hospital, the sound of the big incoming shells stopped. We learned later that morning that our artillery, along with some of our wonderful dive-bombers, had knocked the two railroad guns out of action in Rome. By noon that day, everyone who could be moved was taken out to the Anzio dock to wait for the ship to be unloaded.

They carried me out on a stretcher and set it down on the dock. It was so quiet and peaceful lying there in the sun with the cool breeze blowing in from the sea. By sundown all the wounded were onboard the ship. They carried me aboard and placed me in a bunk below deck. I did not know any of the soldiers there. We got under way at about sundown.

Sometime around midnight I woke up with a sharp pain in my side and cold sweat on my face. I awoke the guy in the next bunk and told him to go to sick bay and bring a medic. By the time he returned with the medic the pain had worsened. He took my temperature, and I had a high fever. He said he had nothing he could give me for pain, but he did stand by and later reported my condition to the captain.

When we docked in Naples the next morning at sunrise, two sailors carried me off of the ship to a waiting ambulance. I was the first one down the gangplank. It was a short ride to the 400th General Hospital in downtown Naples. It was a modern hospital. It was four stories high and was about as large as one of our city blocks. They carried me into the operating room on the third floor where doctors and nurses were waiting for me. They were already scrubbed and in their green surgery clothes.

The next thing I remember is waking up in a hospital bed in

a ward with eleven other soldiers with bandages. The young man across the aisle from me had lost one arm and was also bandaged around the chest like me. A shell from one of those German six-barrel mortars had landed in the foxhole with him. I decided real soon that I had been very lucky. All I had to do was look around the ward and see several guys who were worse than I was. I tried to keep that attitude from that time forward.

A nurse was with me when I awoke. Soon the doctor who performed the surgery came in to see me. He said the place where they had removed part of my lung was full of fluid and was infected. They reopened the wound, cleaned the inside of my chest, and sewed it up again. They continued giving me pain medicine, and I spent the next few days sleeping.

One morning I awoke with a sharp pain in my side again. The nurse said that I had been at the 400th general hospital for a week. They took me to surgery again. This time they x-rayed my chest and took me back to the ward. My doctor came in and told me that the cavity where part of my lung was removed had filled up with fluid again, but that he was going to try another method this time to take the fluid out. He said he would use a needle and syringe and not open the wound.

In a few minutes, the nurse came and gave me a shot in the right side to deaden the area. She left and soon returned with the doctor and the equipment that they would use. A half-gallon shiny pan, a 500cc syringe connected to an 8 inch needle, cut off on the end at a 45 degree angle, and about the size of a soda straw

I had all the confidence in the world in my doctor. After all, I had no other choice. He carefully placed the big needle between two ribs just above my wound and gently pushed it in to the hilt. I watched it go in all the way. I heard several "Oh's" and "Ah's" from the guys in the ward and as I glanced around the room, all heads were turned away from me. The guy in the bed next to mine fainted, and the nurse dashed around the bunk to take care of him. The doctor began drawing the reddish brown fluid into the syringe.

I was sitting up with my back against the headboard. The nurse had been holding my shoulders real tight in case I was unable to watch. The doctor filled the syringe and detached it from the base of the needle, holding it in place. He reached for the pan. The nurse had left it sitting at the foot of my bunk and he could not reach it. I asked the doctor if I could give him a hand, and I placed my left hand under his and took hold of the base of the needle. He was shocked.

He looked me in the eye as if he could not believe that I had offered to hold the needle. Then he smiled and went about emptying the syringe. I had no problem helping the doctor. I could feel no pain and needles never bothered me. He drew another 500cc of fluid from my side before he stopped.

The draining worked well. When the feeling came back in my side I had no pain. Later that day, a patient came in and sat down on my bed. I had never seen him before. His name was J.B. Hood and he said he was from Maysville, Oklahoma, about 10 miles east of Lindsay, my hometown. It was so good to see someone from so close to home even if I did not know him. There were some observation booths around the operating room, and J.B. had watched while they did the surgery on me that first day they brought me in. He said that word had traveled ahead of my arrival, who I was, where I was from, what outfit I was in, and where I was wounded. We had a long talk, and J.B. came to see me every day. He told me that his brother, Bob Hood, was the city marshall of Lindsay. Even though we did not know each other, he knew a lot of people that I knew.

In a few weeks, I began to gain some strength, and had to begin to learn to walk again. I didn't have any more complications, but my whole left side was numb, plumb down to my groin. The next step was to get on a regular diet and walk downstairs to the mess hall.

After three months I was released from the hospital and driven to the dock where about 300 other disabled guys and I boarded a merchant marine ship that was sailing back to the good old U.S.A.

As we sailed toward the Strait of Gibraltar June 4th, we heard a news flash. The American army on the Anzio beachhead had won the Battle of Anzio. They had pushed the German army back and had entered Rome. It was a great day for me. But even though I was so happy for the men who were still fighting there, I knew the war was not over. This was only another milestone in the long, hard road to Germany. It was the first news I had heard about the old 45th since I was carried off on a stretcher that night.

Two days later, we were on the high seas sailing west when we heard another news report. The Allied army had landed in France at Normandy. What a traumatic day that was in the lives of the men who were there! It was the biggest amphibious landing in the history of our country. It took place on beaches that were so well fortified that Hitler thought it was impossible for our army to land there and survive. And survive they did, but with heavy losses of lives and equipment of all kinds from ships and planes to supplies and guns, as history states. Having made three landings on enemy soil I could sympathize with the soldiers who made that landing, but it was far beyond my imagination as to the actual situation there until much later when I learned more about the details. None of the landings that my division made even come close to comparing with the Normandy landing. That landing turned the tide in the war against the Nazis and Adolf Hitler. No one, except those who were there, can comprehend what took place there that day and the days thereafter. The closer the Allied army got to Berlin, Germany, the tougher it was to advance, the more experienced the enemy troops were, and the heavier the losses were.

The Normandy invasion by the allies on June 6th, 1944, in Northern France included 175,000 troops, 11,000 airplanes, 5,000 ships, and countless support groups such as paratroops, supplies, medics, and many more.

Chapter 17
Going Home:
Post War Traumatic Stress Syndrome

The day I learned of the invasion at Normandy I realized that one purpose of our mission in Sicily and on the mainland of Italy had been to make a threat to the south of Germany. They wanted us to draw part of the German army away from the homeland and the north of France where the Normandy landing took place.

In a few days, we arrived in New York Harbor and sailed by the Statue of Liberty. It was much more thrilling this time than seeing it from the train two years before. I was given leave of absence that day to go home and visit my folks. I was to report to Fort Sam Houston in San Antonio in two weeks.

I called my brother Scott, who was in the air force and stationed at the air base near Enid, Oklahoma. I told him I would arrive at the train station in Oklahoma City at a certain time. He and his wife, Toogie, picked me up there and drove me home.

I was so emotional when I saw my brother and his wife I could not keep from crying. I think they understood. As I remember the ride to Lindsay, my hometown was real quiet. I was at a loss about what to say and I guess they were too. I did enjoy the ride and the scenery. We soon arrived at the new farm Dad and Mom had bought, half a mile north of Lindsay. I had been away for five years. When I saw Mom and Dad and my three sisters, Emogene, Fannie, and Lois, I choked up again. The land that I could see was pastureland covered with grass. The farming land was beyond the hill. The house was unfinished. There were no other buildings on the location where they had chosen to build their home. I was so glad that they finally owned their own place after all those years of sharecropping. But mostly I was glad to be back home again.

They took me in the house. It was livable but a long time from being finished. Lunch was ready and how ready I was to eat some of Mom's cooking again. But first, they wanted to see my battle scars. I could understand that. I had managed to send only one V-Mail letter since I was wounded. That was from the hospital in Naples. All V-Mail was censored and all I was allowed to write was that I was in the hospital in Naples and that I loved them. They looked in silence except I heard some "ooh's" and "aah's" when we sat down to Mom's home-cooked meal. To my surprise and disappointment, after a dozen bites I was full. I could not swallow another bite. After a year of K-rations, my stomach must have shrunk. The homemade ice tea tasted good though. I had a hard time explaining to my Mom that I could not eat anything else at that time. She had always insisted that we have some more of this or that. It would be a couple more months before I could eat a normal amount of food at a meal.

Dad was so proud of me. He had been doing a lot of volunteer work and giving what he could afford to the Red Cross, but mostly because I was overseas. He asked me if I had been helped much by the Red Cross, especially while I was over there. I had to tell him the truth. It almost broke his heart when I told him I had not seen the Red Cross over there, not even in the hospital in Naples. The only times I had seen them was at the dance at the U.S.O. clubs near the camps where I was stationed before I went over seas.

Dad wanted to show me off, so the next day he drove me to town. We parked on Main Street and got out of the car. I was wearing my full dress uniform with the red and yellow insignia patch for the thunderbird division on my shoulder. The first person we saw was the Oklahoma State Representative for that area. He was a loud-mouthed local farmer who thought he knew everything. He saw the thunderbird patch I was wearing and without speaking or asking me anything, he began to talk down to me. He told me that I was not supposed to wear the 45th Division patch here in the States when that Division was still fighting overseas. He went into a rage pointing his finger at me, and he would not shut up long enough for me to explain.

I finally got enough! I yelled back at him that he did not know what he was talking about and that I was in the proper uniform. I was so shocked and angry that I did not try to explain anything further than that. And that was the end of my happy homecoming. I did not feel that I needed to defend myself for being in the proper uniform. My thoughts were that the inconsiderate blowhard did not deserve an explanation.

Now my dad was a man of very few words, and I saw him start toward the smart aleck. I told the congressman to "go to hell". If I had been up to full strength I would have taken him on. I put my arm around Dad's shoulder and told him, "Let's go home. That smart aleck is not worth the trouble." We got in the car and went home. My homecoming which had been so sweet had now turned bitter, and my morale had gone to the very bottom.

I did not go back to town again during my two weeks furlough.

But I enjoyed being home with my family. I could get around very well, but I was very weak. I could hardly lift anything with my right arm. My upper right side was very weak. My right side from my waist to my breast and from the middle of my stomach to underneath my arm was numb. I could not feel anything in that area. I did not know it then, but in the next few months that numb spot would grow smaller gradually and would disappear after about a year, when the normal feeling returned.

I spent time every day looking over Dad and Mom's new farm. The walking helped me regain some strength, helped me to sleep at night, and helped me improve my appetite. I could hardly believe that, after all these years of share cropping, they finally owned their own farm, and they would never have to move again. They had a home of their own. The house had been an 8th grade schoolhouse close to Elmore City. Dad bought it and had it moved to their farm. It needed quite a bit of repair. My Uncle Ike was busy putting in partitions, working on plumbing, and building a bathroom, a kitchen cabinet, and a front porch. The fences also needed rebuilding and there were no barns or outbuildings. I felt bad that I was unable to help.

Dad had a herd of about 30 cattle. On Sunday he walked through the pasture with me. He pointed out two cows and two calves and a fine yearling heifer and told me they were all mine. They were the increase from that one little tiny heifer calf that Dad had given to me when I was in high school, the one I held up so it could nurse. He said there had been two bull-calves born, and that he had sold them and put the money into my account. I had been away five years and all that time Dad had taken care of my herd.

After two weeks I reported to the army hospital in San Antonio. They were expecting me, and they had my records. The next several days I had all kinds of tests and examinations including x-rays. I saw for the first time an x-ray of my right lung with the bottom half missing and the fourth rib on that side was gone except for a tiny short stub at my back bone and another short stub at my breast bone. That didn't bother me as much as being weak and not being able to do anything. I had been active all of my life and now this.

I read that First Lady Eleanor Roosevelt had recommended to Congress that they should set up or create a rehabilitation center for all veterans that were returning home from a war zone. They would require them to stay there two or three months for therapy before their return home or their re-entry or exposure to society. When I considered what happened to me on my first trip to town when I returned home, I thought it would be a mighty good thing. Every day and every night I relived some of the things that had happened to me or to some of my dear friends overseas while we were in battle. I slept very little. When I did fall asleep I usually had a nightmare and jumped up screaming. I thought about my friends who were with me when they were killed. I thought about those guys' families who would never see them again. Then I thought how lucky I was to be alive and back in the good old U.S. of A.

The hospital released me to the Fort Sam Houston Veterans Rehab Center and gave me an appointment to return to the hospital in 30 days for a check-up. I asked for a furlough and returned home.

After a few days, I got so bored that I went into town. Lindsay had not changed much in the five years that I had been away. Main Street was still three blocks long from the rail depot to the city jail. It was about the same as when I was a young boy going to town on Saturday afternoon to help my Mother sell her eggs and cream and to help her buy the groceries and carry them to the wagon or the old Model T truck. There still was nothing to do in Lindsay during the weekdays. The theaters only opened to show the Saturday evening matinee, then the Saturday night feature, then the late show called the preview, which started about 10 p.m.

I walked the three blocks up and back and did not see anything different or exciting. Then I turned into the pool hall where my cousin Albert and I used to shoot pool on Saturday nights while we waited for the preview to start. There were four or five young men that I knew in the poolroom. They were all about my age. They began to ask strange things about the army in general, about what it was like in the battle zone, and whether it hurt when I got shot. One even asked me how many Germans I had killed. I realized real quick that none of them had been in the service, and that they were insensitive to my feelings. At first I tried to be honest and informative with my answers. When I got a chance I blurted out the question "Have any of you been in the armed forces?" I got a lot of carefully worded answers after a short silence, like, "No, I got a deferment to help out on my old man's farm." Another said, "Yeah, me too." Another said he took some stuff to increase his pulse rate when he took his physical and failed it.

I tried not to let it bother me too much, but the fact that they were happy about what they had done disgusted me. These guys seemed to think that war was all fun and games; thrills and excitement. Yet, they evidently wanted no part of it. I was surprised and amused that this type of attitude existed in the minds of young, able-bodied American men. One guy asked me what it was like to kill a German soldier. The Moore boy said he hoped the war lasted a long time so his daddy could make lots more money.

I decided that nothing I could say or do would change their ideas about the war. I knew one thing for sure, though. I did not want any of these guys for friends, so I quickly withdrew from the pool hall and went back to the house and my family.

Chapter 18
Home – What To Do?

My little sisters had grown so much in the last five years. Lois had not started to school when I left for college. Fannie started to school when I was in my senior year in high school. It was good to be around them. They were both going to school at Lindsay High School. Fannie and Dad liked to play pitch. It seemed that Fannie won almost every game. Dad wore glasses and it turned out, on a closer look, that Fannie could see his cards in the reflection of them. I never mentioned that to Dad as long as he lived. I just let it be our little secret. Lois and Fannie were always together if it was at all possible. When you saw one, the other one was right there.

One day, Dad let me disc-plow some ground with the old Case tractor. It seemed like old times. Dad had mounted a seat from a cultivator on each fender of the tractor so the girls could ride with Dad when he drove the tractor. Each seat faced the driver. The girls came along with me that day that I plowed and rode in their seats. After awhile, I drove under some low branches on a tree without thinking. Lois was about to be swept off of her seat so she grabbed the branch. Before I could see what was happening, the branch lifted her off her seat and she dropped to the ground in front of the disc. By the time I realized what happened and stopped the tractor, the disc had caught her leg enough to break the skin. She was not hurt otherwise but I felt very bad about it. I should have been more careful but I was so glad I was able to stop in time.

One night it came a flood. Floodwater was waist deep in the road by the bridge between Dad's house and town. When the girls were ready for school that morning, Dad saddled his pony, old Starlight, and carried the girls behind the saddle. The horse waded across the long stretch of floodwater and carried them to school.

Dad had started building a barn and corral and had plans to build a chicken house and a washhouse for Mom. I began to do what I could to help Dad with his building. It helped me pass the time and the exercise helped me to gain strength and to sleep better at night. Dad never said whether I was much help to him. I just did what I could.

My older sister, Emogene, lived there with Mom and Dad while her husband, J.B. Reynolds, was away in the armed forces somewhere in Burma with General Stillwell. Emogene was two years older than I was and we were very close while we were growing up. She was a no-nonsense person while I liked to kid around. My Mom and Dad would not put up with any "tomfoolery", but I liked to pull little harmless pranks.

Emogene was nicknamed "Bill" by my Dad. I guess he was hoping for another boy when she was born. My two older brothers would rub my nose in the sand if I tried any silly stuff on them, and "Bill" would get the broom after me in a minute. She was left-handed so I never knew which way she was coming, left or right, but she could "clean my lister" every time. She played basketball at old Hughes High. That was way back when the elderly women were all upset because the girls were playing in basketball trunks. Even though the pant legs reached almost to their knees. "Bill" was a good player and could fool every opponent with that left-handed hook shot. That was a long time ago when girl's basketball had just started. Scholarships didnt exist for girls so she never had a chance to go to college. If she had gone, I think she would have made a really good basketball player. On the other hand, she and I hoed many a row of corn and cotton every spring and summer while my Dad and brothers did the plowing so it was good that she was there. Elizabeth "Toogie" Price-Worley, who married my oldest brother Scott, also joined us in the corn and cotton fields and helped us with the hoeing. Toogie was like a sister to me.

Scott went into the air force and was stationed at Enid, Oklahoma. He was an airplane mechanic and a certified welder. Seburn had signed up with a big contractor and was in the Aleutian Islands helping to build a huge airport. He was a heavy-duty mechanic and worked on Caterpillars, cranes, draglines, and that sort of thing. As I said before, all of my friends went overseas to Italy. Some of them were buried at Anzio, some at Salerno, and others were still fighting the Germans somewhere north of Rome. Soon they would be making another amphibious landing on the beaches of southern France, then moving on into Germany.

When my furlough was up I returned to San Antonio and went to the hospital. I made my appointment and the doctor was pleased with my improvement. I had done so well that he released me from the hospital. I was assigned to the Reassignment Center at Fort Sam Houston. I was to have another check-up in thirty days. In a couple of weeks, I was transferred to Camp Crowder, Missouri, to a recruit training center. I was assigned to a platoon made up of war veterans and recruits. I was not assigned as a platoon sergeant, but as a recruit. They had permanent drill sergeants there. We did close order drill six hours a day. I was happy that I was strong enough to do that.

In two weeks, the appointment for my next check-up came due. I was ordered to check into the hospital. I was there a week, lying around, having a test or an examination each day. On Friday the doctor came to my room and told me I was doing fine. Then out of the clear blue he said he was discharging me from the army and that I was to report to the admitting office as soon as I changed clothes. When I reported, they had already filled out my papers, and had them ready for me to sign. I could see then that the doctor had arranged everything before he came to my room.

I was a little shook up, but I tried not to show any emotion, which was something I had learned with my buddies the last five years. This was so unexpected, so sudden. I felt like I had been blind-sided. Since I had been at Camp Crowder, I had been trying to guess where they would send me: the Normandy beachhead in France, the South Pacific, or maybe back to my old outfit, the 45th Division, which was then fighting in southern France and Germany. Being discharged had never entered my mind. Along with being a little shocked, I was also disappointed. It gave me a whole new look at my future. My hopes of ever making a career of the Army were immediately lost. It had been seven months since I was wounded and five years since I enlisted in the National Guard but it took only a few minutes to muster me out. I walked out of the office, down the hall, and out the door. I asked for directions to the bus station. There was a bus ready to leave for Tulsa and within an hour I was on that bus and on my way home.

I tried to sleep on the bus, but that didn't work. So I did a lot of thinking instead. What was I going to do now? My folks didn't even know that I had been transferred to Camp Crowder. I rode the bus to Miami, Oklahoma, and got off there. I looked up an old friend who lived there, Joe Booth, and spent the night. Joe was in my company at Fort Sill and Camp Barkley. He was one swell guy. His pretty young wife moved to Abilene while we were at Camp Barkley and had their first and only child, a beautiful baby boy. She died of leukemia soon after the baby was born so Joe took an emergency discharge and took his young son home to Miami to raise. It was so good to see Joe and the boy. Joe had not remarried. His Dad and Mom had been helping him raise his son, but they had passed away a couple of years earlier, so he was raising his son by himself on his parents' home farm and farming the land. We had a real nice visit, then I left for Lindsay.

It was good to be home again. It would take a while to get used to the idea that I would not be going back to the army. Dad and Mother welcomed me with open arms. I guess they were more worried about me going back overseas than I could imagine.

I was strong enough by then to be a little more help to Dad. We finished the barn. It had one room for grain and feed, one for hay, and a shed large enough to milk a couple or three cows under. We built a fine corral about 6 feet high, a chicken house for Mom's hens, and a washhouse. The old two-story Hughes schoolhouse burned down back in 1934, and Scott and Seburn helped tear down the old brick walls. They were given some of the bricks for helping to haul the rest of them off, which I used to lay a red brick walk from the back door of the house to the corral. All of these buildings are still standing to this day. The hen house and washhouse are not used anymore and the hen house has since been moved a few feet south.

There was a little history about the farm. There was a hill which was covered with short grass, just north of the house. It was also covered with prairie dogs and their dens. On top of the prairie dog hill was the remains of an old ranch house that had been burned long ago. There was a dry, old dug well that was left uncovered. The old rock foundation was mostly scattered and old pieces of tin, rusty metal, and pieces of plows were scattered everywhere. That had been the homestead of the Story family, about the turn of the century, before Oklahoma's statehood. The word was that one of the Story boys was a mean outlaw and was killed on the front porch of the old home.

Now, cattle and horses had been known to break their legs when they stepped in a prairie dog hole, and the prairie dogs also ate a lot of the grass up on that hill. So Dad decided he wanted to get rid of the varmints and he heard somewhere that a product called Hi-Life would do the trick. Now, Hi-Life was very potent. It would burn your nostrils if you were to smell it and it evaporated quickly. In this day and time, the environmentalists would hang us for using anything like it. But we had not heard of such an organization back then, so Dad bought a gallon of Hi-Life. We soaked corncobs in it, and Dad would throw a cob in a hole, and I would quickly shovel in the loose dirt around the mound until the hole was stopped up, trapping the fumes inside. I would guess there were over a thousand holes so it took us several days to finish the job. When we had completed the job, there were no more prairie dogs!

As long as I stayed busy, I did pretty well. One day, Dad and I were building a fence when we heard that President Roosevelt had died. No one lives forever. When God decides we have finished our purpose here on earth, then we die, but I guess I had thought he would go on living forever. When we finished the building and my work slowed down I began to get restless. The days and weeks became long and I had no friends. I guess you could say I hit an all-time low.

I needed to decide what I was going to do. I only had the last army pay I received and the $300.00 severance that they gave me. I knew that would be gone soon and I was not one to live at home with my Dad and Mom. I did not have a girlfriend. The only things that I knew how to do really well were soldiering, farm work, and some knowledge I had learned from my older brothers about overhauling farm machinery. The Veteran's Education Bill had not been passed yet or even created. My Dad offered to pay me back the money he had borrowed from me to buy the farm or he would sign half of the farm over to my name and we would farm it together. I told him that was a real generous offer. Five years before, when I graduated from high school, he had offered to make me his partner in sharecropping. I told him then that I would like to try something besides farming. I told him the same thing this time, too. I knew that Dad did not have the money to pay me back. Oh, he could have borrowed the money against the farm, but that would have put him at risk and there were several people in the area that wanted that farm. Harry Moore told Dad if he had known the farm was for sale, Dad would never have had a chance to buy it. I told Dad I would look around and try to decide what I would like to do and for him not to worry about paying me anything. I wanted Dad and Mom to have that home and farm so bad that I did not want anything to stand in the way.

My friends, the ones who were still alive and still over there fighting, would have said to me, "How lucky can you get? You are alive and you are home." We had talked many times about buddies who, like myself, were wounded badly enough that they were sent home and lived. We called it the "million dollar wound". But when we were joking about it, I never thought it would happen to me, nor did I dream that it would be so lonely and boring.

As I said, I did pretty well as long as I was doing something with Dad there on the farm. It was so good to eat Mother's cooking again. And it was fun to be around the girls again. But I soon became so bored that I bought a bottle of whiskey one Saturday night and, against my better judgment, I took a few sips. I never liked the taste of alcohol, and I am so thankful for that. Here I was, taking something into my mouth that gagged me, even though I hated being around drunks in the army! I would take a few sips on Saturday night while waiting for the late show to start at the old Blue Moon Theater.

Most drunks did one of two things. Some would cry on your shoulder, tell you how much they liked you, and tell you their troubles. The others wanted to fight. I didn't drink much and I never got out of control, but it is always dangerous to fool around with any kind of alcohol or drugs, or even tobacco. They are so addictive. Drugs were not around much in those days and I am thankful for that. I am ashamed that I did this before my Mom and Dad. They were kind enough that they never said anything, but they knew.

On Saturday night after a few snorts of whiskey, I wanted to talk about my experiences in the war. To my disappointment, no one wanted to hear about them. Most people would change the subject; some would walk away; some did not believe me and even said so. As time went by I became less and less outgoing. I became a loner and decided to just keep things to myself.

When my money was almost all gone I met a guy named Dow Tipton. He had checked into my background and offered me a job helping him overhaul some heavy equipment. He had bought two Caterpillars, a dump truck and a front-end loader on a Ford tractor from an army surplus sale. All of them needed major repairs. Dow was trying to start a small dirt moving company. The army was selling off a lot of their equipment rather than repairing it. I took the job. I decided that I could do the job allright with my experience from working on old cars, farm machinery, tractors, threshing machines, broomcorn balers, hay balers, and so on. Dow had rented an old service station, one block from Main Street in Lindsay, and we started overhauling the dump truck the next day.

CHAPTER 19
The Happy Years

One Saturday night I went into the Lindsay Cafe for a hamburger before going to the late night show. There was a small dance floor in the back room. Music was playing back there so I walked back to take a look. People were dancing. And to my surprise, all of them were nice, young people.

At first I did not see anyone I knew, but they all knew who I was. As I glanced around the room I saw a face that looked familiar. It was the prettiest girl I ever saw in my life. She had a nice, smooth tan; brown eyes; sparkling white teeth; and a smile as bright as the sunrise. I remembered seeing this young lady five years ago at the Lindsay High School gymnasium. She was a Lindsay High School cheerleader, and I was a Hughes High School senior playing my last high school basketball game against Lindsay. I did not know her name; but she was pretty then and prettier now. I strolled over and asked if she would go to the late night show with me. She said she would. So we went. There was not much to do in Lindsay except go to the show and go to one of the cafes for a Coke and a hamburger. She said she was not seeing anyone on a regular basis. So I asked if I could see her again, and she said that would be okay with her. I knew then that I would be back.

The army surplus sales were held at army camps in Oklahoma, Texas, and Louisiana about once a month. Dow took me with him to these sales to help him select the best bargains from the equipment that was displayed for sale. This provided me with plenty of work. When I finished the first truck, there was another one with the clutch out on it. Then there was an R5 Caterpillar that needed new clutches in both sides. When I had finished the Caterpillar I took time to try it out. I smoothed up the driveway and the area around the shop. Dow hired an operator and put him to building a farm pond for a farmer. We were in business. Dow was a good manager. He soon lined up enough farm ponds and levies to keep the Caterpillar busy for a year at least. So we went to another surplus sale and Dow bought another Caterpillar. This one only needed some minor tune-up work. When I got it ready to go, Dow put me to operating it at building a levy for a farmer south of town and the work kept coming.

The nice young lady that went with me to the show that night worked at the Ben Franklin "Five and Dime" store known then as the variety store. Her name was Mary Imogene Pelton. I went to the store on Main Street and asked her for a date. She told me we had to talk. I thought, "Oh no, she has another boyfriend." But I managed to say "OK." She told me that if I wanted to date her, I would have to choose between her and the booze. That was not a

hard decision to make. I wanted to be with that young Christian girl very much. I told her that would not be a hard thing for me to do. I went home and poured the whiskey out and threw the bottle away. I wish that I could convince all people, young and old, that alcohol or drugs is not the solution to their troubles. Those things are only a temporary relief, and could quickly lead to addiction. In this day and time I hear and read about a lot of folks who try drugs and/or alcohol because of peer pressure, or do it on a dare by someone. Some people want to be like everyone else and they use the excuse, "Everybody is doing it." How sad that is. In my whole life I was never persuaded to do something just because someone else was doing it. I guess it was because I wanted to be my own self. I give all the credit for that to my Dad, my Mom, and my brothers and sisters. My brothers gave me confidence in myself, and that confidence is what it takes to stay on your own level and not stoop to someone else's. Every type of problem or trouble, no matter how big, can be solved without using alcohol or drugs. All you have to do is call on the Almighty God and have faith in Him and He will give you a solution. I guarantee anyone will be a better person without the use of drugs or alcohol. If I had not believed in God I would not be here today.

Still, I was troubled with the memories of war and the loss of my friends who died over there. I soon began to believe that if I did not talk about my troubles that they would soon be forgotten. Little did I know that it worked just the opposite. There were so many people who did not want to hear about the war, so I quit bringing it up on my own. I could talk about my troubles to Dad, Mom, and my brothers and sisters, and they would listen. But I did not want to burden them too much.

Miss Mary Imogene Pelton and I were soon dating steadily, and that was the best thing that had ever happened to me, and that was the best decision I ever made in my lifetime. It put me back on track and gave me some new goals for my life and some hope for good things in the future.

We usually went out every Saturday night. I liked her very much. She understood me more than anyone else did. We usually went to the late night show and had a hamburger and Coke afterwards. Sometimes we would double date with Buddy Cherry and Louise Spradlin, who went to school at Lindsay with Imogene. Buddy was a

Mary Imogene Pelton

lariat rope performer and performed at hospitals and rodeos and the like. Imogene was a very bright and good-looking girl with a good outlook on life and a good sense of humor. She was a lot of fun. I also liked her family. Her Mom, Mary Pelton, and I always got along well. Her Dad and I also got along well. Mr. Marion Pelton was a painter and paperhanger. Lindsay citizens kept him a lot busier than he wanted to be because he loved to fish. Sometimes he fished in some farm pond, but most of the time he fished in the Washita River that ran near Lindsay. Her brother, Clarence, was a couple of years older than she was, and he was away in the Merchant Marines. Her sister, Anna Lou, was nine years younger than she was and was in school at Lindsay High. Her mother was a Clingman before she married Mr. Pelton, and had three sisters and eleven brothers. All but two of the aunts and uncles were married, and most of them worked in the oilfield. It took me at least two years to learn all of their names and which spouse belonged to whom.

Christmas came and went. I don't remember much about it except that it was the first Christmas I had spent with my parents in four years. It brought back memories of the year before when we spent Christmas on the front lines, high up in the mountains northeast of Naples, Italy. It was bitter cold. We were dug in. We had reached a German defense that we could not break. They had brought our Christmas dinner on pack mules. It was then that I thought I saw Dad's little red mule, Snip, in that pack mule train.

During my first day home when I came back from overseas, I was walking through the pasture looking at Dad's cattle. I did not see old Snip, so I asked my brother where Dad's little red mule was. He told me that Dad had sold her because he did not need her to do the plowing after he bought the tractor and because he couldn't ride her because she was never broke to ride. So he sold her and bought a saddle horse named Starlight. My brother told me Dad had sold 'Old Snip' to a man who was buying small mules for the army. They were to be shipped to Italy to be used for pack mules to carry supplies up in the mountains to the soldiers. This is how I found out that it really was old Snip that Christmas in Italy. This is a good example for young boys and girls why they should never keep secrets from their parents. I remember I was so emotional about finding this out that I cried. If dad had known that his pet mule could be ridden I know he never would have given her up.

The following spring Imogene and I decided to get married. On a Monday morning I had to go to Oklahoma City for some Caterpillar parts. While I was there, I went by the courthouse and purchased our marriage license. I did not know that we would have to get married in the same county where I bought the license. I read that part after I got home. I had been building a farm pond way down southeast of Hughes School on Rush Creek. When Saturday evening came I rolled the old Caterpillar up on a high place and left for home. After I bathed and dressed, I told my folks what we were going to do, and went to pick up Imogene and we told her folks.

We went to the late night show at the old Blue Moon Theater. Then we drove to Oklahoma City. We found a Justice of the Peace, woke him up, and he married us at his house. His wife was the witness.

Colbert & Evelyn Starr

We then started out for Enid, Oklahoma, where Scott and Toogie lived. After we arrived, we found out that Scott was being shipped overseas that afternoon. We went down to the train station with Toogie and Scott, and saw him off. We stayed with Toogie for about a week, then headed for Arkansas for a few days where Colbert Starr lived with his folks. Colbert had survived his terrible wounds. He had several pieces of shrapnel removed from his lung and his left arm was torn up so bad between the shoulder and elbow that he had no use of it. His arm and hand just hung loose from his shoulder.

We stayed with them a week and when our money was about all gone, we went back to Lindsay to see if we still had our jobs and to start our new life together.

We moved in for a short time with Imogene's mom and dad where Imogene's Mom fixed up their back bedroom into a little one-room apartment. Our jobs had not been taken so I went back to work for Dow Tipton and Imogene went back to work in the five and dime store. We began to make plans about where to live, what to do, how to manage our money and all of the other things newlyweds must work through. We were so thankful for Imogene's parents and were in no hurry to move out. They made us feel welcome as long as we wanted to stay there but we soon knew we had to get on with our lives, so we moved on.

We dedicated ourselves to making a happy home for our children, (since we would eventually have four) and our lives and experiences together have been so happy that I think it would make a good book. But that is another story that I hope to put on paper someday.

Over 50 years of my life went by before I finally realized that keeping depressing things to yourself will never work to make them go away. I mostly learned this from reading Colonel David Hackworth's book, _About Face_. When I was finally encouraged enough to begin talking about some of the things that happened to me during the war I found it was not as hard as I thought it would be. I was even able to get through some of the painful memories of my buddies who were killed in action without crying. Some of my dearest friends and fellow soldiers died over there fighting for our great country, Mom, Dad, and apple pie, so I finally decided that if Colonel Hackworth could reveal his war experiences, then I could too, and everything worked out for the best after all.

I believe that everyone can enjoy life if you don't let little things get you down, don't dwell on things in the past or worry about things you can do nothing about. Instead, have faith in God, and repent and ask His forgiveness for your sins. Have a positive attitude, watch for the pitfalls in life, keep your eye on your goals, and believe that God is the all-knowing, all-seeing God that brought us into this world, and trust Him that He loves you and knows where you are and what you're going through no matter what happens in life. He will determine how long we are going to live here anyway, so live for Him and be happy.

Recently the government has made it illegal to display the Ten Commandments in a public building such as a courthouse or school building. It is also illegal for a person to lead a prayer at a public gathering such as a football game or any other assembly for athletics. They say the prayers infringe upon some people's first amendment rights. A lot of Christian people have been really upset over this issue.

This year a couple of teenage students stood before the school board in their district and asked if it would be all right to have a "moment of silence" before the beginning of a sports game. I am so proud of them. What a brilliant idea to bypass an issue that has been so controversial. I personally do not believe that someone has to pray in public over a loud speaker for their prayers to be answered. A person can pray silently the way he or she wants to and the way they believe. I have prayed many silent prayers. I have prayed many times when there was no "person" there to hear my prayer. I believe in God, and I believe He answers prayers because He answered my prayers. If he had not answered some of them, I would not be here, alive today.

John B. Worley
2002

John Worley-1944

Some of the Author's Favorite Poems

This is in memory of my Mom, Dad and two older brothers.

God saw you were getting tired
    and a cure was not to be.
So He put his arms around you
    and whispered, "Come with me".
A golden heart stopped beating
    and I watched you fade away
Although I love you dearly,
    I could not make you stay.
In the stillness of the night
    GOD put hard working hands to rest.
He broke my heart to prove to me
    that he only takes the best.
It's lonesome here without you.
    I miss you more each day.
Life doesn't seem the same
    since you went away.
When days are sad and lonely;
    and everything goes wrong,
I seem to hear you whisper,
    "Cheer up and carry on".
Each time I see your picture,
    you seem to smile and say,
"Don't cry, you are in GOD's hands.
    We will meet again some day.

Below is one of the poems that I memorized
in a contest in 8th grade. It always made me feel
a little sad, but it has always been one of my favorites.

Little Boy Blue

The little toy dog is covered with dust;
    But sturdy and staunch he stands.
And the little toy soldier is red with rust,
    And his musket moulds in his hands.

Time was when the little toy dog was new,
    And the soldier was passing fair.
And that was the time when our Little Boy Blue,
    Kissed them and put them there.

"Now, don't you go till I come," he said,
    "And don't you make any noise!"
So, toddling off to his trundle-bed,
    He dreamt of the pretty toys;

And, as he was dreaming, an angel song
    Awakened our Little Boy Blue--
Oh! The years are many, the years are long,
    But the little toy friends are true!

Ay, faithful to Little Boy Blue they stand,
    Each in the same old place--
Awaiting the touch of a little hand,
    The smile of a little face;

And they wonder, as waiting the long years through
    In the dust of that little chair,
What has become of our Little Boy Blue,
    Since he kissed them and put them there.
                    -Eugene Fields (1850-1895)

This Jangle was composed by the Author

A – lways respect your parents and love them.
L – ook for the good things in life.
W – alk away from temptation.
A – wake each day with a clear conscience.
Y – ou hold your destiny in your own hands.
S – ave your love for your life long sweetheart.

B – elieve on the Lord of Lords,
    Who made the universe.
E – nvy no one, but respect their good deeds.

T – hank God daily for your blessings.
R – espect and obey the laws of the land.
U – se your head; don't do anything stupid.
T – ell your parents, your teacher, or a friend
    when someone bullies you.
H – ave no part in gangs or with evil kids.
F – ill your life with joy instead of sorrow.
U – se caution when someone dares you
    to do something wrong.
L – eave drugs, alcohol, and tobacco alone.

When illness stays our busy pace
    and sets our plans aside:
Remember in that stillness,
    Gods spirit does abide.
And when we listen closely
    in the quietness we hear
The almost silent voice of God
    and know that He is near.
                -Richard R. Smith

I Love To Live

(This was given to me by my good friends Buddy &
Shirley West and Velma England,on my 80th birthday.)

Today, dear Lord, I am 80
and there is much I haven't done.
I hope, dear Lord, you'll let me live until I'm 81.

But then, if I haven't finished all I want to do,
Would you please let me live until I'm 82?

So many places I want to go, so very much to see,
Do you think that You could manage to make it 83?

The world is changing very fast; there is so much in store,
I'd like it very much to live until I'm 84.
And if by then I'm still alive, I'd like to stay until 85!

More plans will be up in the air, so I'd really like to stick
around to see what happens to the world when I turn 86.

I know, dear Lord, it's much to ask
and it must be nice in heaven,
But I'd really like to stay until I turn 87.

I know by then I won't be fast and sometimes will be late,
But it would sure be pleasant to be around at 88.

I will have seen so many things and had a wonderful time,
So, I'm sure that I'll be willing to leave at the age of 89...

Maybe just one more thing I'd like to say,
Dear Lord, I thank you kindly,
But if it's okay with You, I'd love to live past 90.

-Author Unknown

Thanksgiving Every Day

Even though I clutch my blanket
and growl when my alarm rings.
    "Thank you, Lord, that I can hear"
    – there are many that are deaf.

Even though I keep my eyes closed
against the morning light,
    "Thank you, Lord, that I can see"
    – for many are blind.

Even though I put off getting up until later.
    "Thank you, Lord, that I can rise"
    – some folks are bedridden.

Even my first hour is hectic
when toast is burned, kids are loud
and tempers are short.
    "Thank you, Lord for my family"
    – there are many that are lonely.

Even though our breakfast meal
may not be a balanced diet,
    "Thank you, Lord for the food we have"
    – there are many that are hungry.

Even though my job is sometimes monotonous,
    "Thank you, Lord for the opportunity to work"
    – there are many that have no job.

Even though I grumble from day to day
and wish circumstances were not so modest,
    "Thank you, Lord for Life."

If we can pass this on to most people we know,
It might help to make the world a better place to live.